# Insights into Literary Theory

*The 'greatness' of literature cannot be determined solely by literary standards; though we must remember that whether it is literature or not can be determined only by literary standards.*

**T S Eliot**

# Insights into Literary Theory:
## Eastern and Western Perspectives

R P Sharma

GYAN

GYAN PUBLISHING HOUSE

New Delhi 110 002

INSIGHTS INTO LITERARY THEORY:
EASTERN AND WESTERN PERSPECTIVES
[*Literature, Psychology*]

ISBN : 81-212-0534-4



Published in 1996 in India by
Gyan Publishing House
5, Ansari Road
New Delhi 110 002



Laser Typeset at Akshar, Delhi
Printed at Mehra Offset Press, New Delhi

# Contents

# Preface

As a systematic theory of creative writing, Poetics (*Kavyashastra* in Sanskrit) studies the various forms, techniques and resources of literature and seeks to define its nature and function. The theoretical nature of this discipline derives its justification from its eternal concern with formulating the principles and criteria of judgements of literariness. It proceeds from the general to the particular in order that the latter may be properly situated and appreciated. Aristotle defines it as a science that deals with "poetry itself and its kinds and the specific power of each, the way in which the plot is to be constructed if the poem is to be beautiful, of how many and of what parts it is composed, and anything else which falls within the same inquiry" (*Poetics*, Chapter 1). In Sanskrit *Sahitya-Vidya* was originally used to designate the theory of literature but in course of time *Kavyashastra* came to be established as *the* term for the systematic study of creative writings in general. Kavyashastra, like Greek Poetics, deals with the nature and function of literature as a separate and separable form of human creativity. Kavyashastra, like Poetics, has, over the centuries, passed through several detours and given rise to a variety of schools of thought to answer questions like `What is Literature' and `What does Literature do'? These various schools of thought have addressed such questions from their respective points of view. It may not be easy for a student of poetics to place these schools of thought in an order of merit but it should not be difficult for anyone to share the traditional view that literary theories like the theory of Rasa and the theory of Catharsis constitute the foundations of poetics. Likewise, the theory of Decorum or Auchitya still deserves to be seen as one of the constitutive theories of poetics.

The history of poetics has created and preserved a variety of literary theories. M H Abrams (1965) distinguishes, in his well-known encyclopedia article, the extant discourses on literature into four types and calls them: *mimetic theories*, which focus attention on the 'relationship' between the text and the world it represents; *pragmatic* theories, which focus attention on the 'instrumentality' of the text in achieving certain effects in the reader; *expressive* theories, which focus attention on the text as an 'elaboration' of the entity known as the 'writer'; and *objective* theories, which focus attention on the 'text' itself as an autonomous, self-contained construct. Abrams' scheme is, no doubt, a critical survey of all the important turns and twists of poetics from Platonism to New Criticism. And yet, there are a number of recent developments in poetics which happen to be outside this scheme. Most of such theories are postmodernist theories but none of them is as challenging and bothersome to the tradition-bound student of poetics as is the theory of *deconstruction*, generally associated with the name of the French philosopher Jacques Derrida, who draws such a sharp line of division between the 'metaphysical' tradition in Western philosophy and the deconstructionist model.

Derrida contends that the Western tradition of thought has always tried to establish certainty and truth by denying or repressing the limitless instability of language. The 'phonocentric' view of the primacy of speech over writing and the 'logocentric' insistence on the certainty of meaning, Derrida contends, are never supported by the nature of language. Drawing on Saussure's view that 'language is a system of differences without positive terms', Derrida argues that the 'differences' that are believed to make the signs meaningful do in fact keep them from meaning anything definite. By coining a French portmanteau word *differance* which combines 'difference' with 'deferral', Derrida seeks to show that the differential nature of meanings in language ceaselessly defers or postpones any determinate meaning: language is an endless chain or 'play of differences' which logocentric discourses vainly try to fix to some original or final term that can never be reached. Deconstructive readings track down within a text the *aporia* or internal contradiction that undermines its claims to coherent meaning. A text can be seen to be deconstructing itself. Deconstruction seeks to subvert not only 'the metaphysical presence of meaning'; it subverts itself. It questions its own questioning; it is sceptical of itself. Meaning in a text, Derrida would say, is indeterminate and undecidable. It is this philosophy of self-scepticism that encourages his critics to charge him with dogmatic nihilism and wilful obscurity. According to his detractors, Derrida is an absolutist without absolutes, a teacher of the science of nescience, a double-dealer in language who writes and speaks a lot even though he does not believe that a text can ever mean anything.

Since literature is a transaction between a human author and a human reader, both of whom believe that language can and does convey meaning, a seeker of literary meaning cannot go with deconstructive theorists because to go with them would mean indulging in a game of undoing literary texts. Poetics is concerned with the making and interpretation of texts. It is therefore important for a student of poetics to turn back, ignoring the babel of deconstructive voices, to those philosophers and theorists who show the way to a better understanding of literature. It is in a context like this that theorists like Freud and Jung become indispensable to poetics.

Freudian and Jungian approaches to literature have obvious and serious limitations; neither of them can ever be treated as a viable theory of literature. But we have to have in mind that a literary text is also a dialogue between two bodies, not merely between two systems of intelligence. Besides, there is a definite connection between desire and figuration, as there is between the texture of the conscious and the dynamics of the unconscious. This connection naturally calls for a mechanism to decipher itself and this mechanism is best offered by a study that looks into the workings of the human mind. Freud and Jung, despite their differences, tell us a great deal about the workings of the human mind. When the psychic history of an artist is rigorously explored in terms of the compulsive images and figures which structure his work, Freudian and Jungian studies of literary texts make fascinating reading.

These papers make an attempt to stretch poetics to an extent that it can formulate a set of criteria to identify 'literariness' even outside literature 'proper'. Literature need not be a monopoly of 'literary' writers alone. People outside the 'profession' can sometimes produce pieces of writing which may turn out to be excellent works of creative literature or of literary theory. Isn't it interesting that even Aristotle was not a literary professional?

*Insights into Literary Theory: Eastern and Western Perspectives* could take the form of a book due to the co-operation and encouragement of my friend, Shri R C Pandey, CIEFL, Shillong and my daughter, Renu. I thank Shri Pandey for his insightful suggestions and his generous library support when I wrote these papers. I thank Renu for her patient and hard work in copying several drafts of each paper at the time of writing as well as for her insistence in recent months that I must publish these papers in one volume. I thank Dr N P Goel, NEHU, Shillong for proof reading the typescript of this volume. I also thank my friends, colleagues and students in NEHU as well as the other members of my family for their affection and support in various forms.

Professor D Thakur, University of Sana's, Sana'a, Republic of Yemen has been so affectionate and kind to me over the years. I owe so much to him. I consider it a privilege that he has written the Introduction to this volume. I take this opportunity to acknowledge my profound sense of gratitude to him for all that he has done for me as well as for the Introduction.

*Department of English* **R P Sharma**
*NEHU, Shillong*
*March 1996*

# Acknowledgements

Grateful acknowledgements are due to the editors and publishers of the following journals for publishing these papers for the first time:

*Journal of Oriental Research*, Madras, 1986-92 for 'Auchitya and Decorum: Parallel Developments in Poetics', *Dibrugarh University Journal of English Studies*, Dibrugarh, 1991 for 'The Jungian Mystique of Literature' and *The North-Eastern Hill University Journal of Social Sciences and Humanities*, NEHU, Shillong, October-December 1985, and October-December 1986 for 'Rasa and Catharsis: Intersecting Theories of Aesthetic Pleasure', and 'The Freudian Paradigm of Literature', respectively.

# Introduction

The papers in this book on poetics can be divided into two groups. In the first group of papers the author examines certain concepts in Sanskrit poetics in relation to parallel concepts in the Graeco-Roman tradition of scholarship. In the second group of papers he discusses literary theory in relation to psycho-analysis. My introduction, therefore, has two parts in it. The first part is intended to make some introductory observations on the papers on Sanskrit poetics and the second part is intended to make certain observations on the author's critical survey of the contribution made to poetics by Freud and Jung.

## I

### 1. Comparing Two Alien Traditions: Need for Precaution

1.1 *Exfluence and Influence*

One of the problems in discussions of this type arises out of the uncertain and fluid meaning of the word "influence", a word which can mean too much in certain situations and too little in certain others. Here, therefore, I would like to differentiate between influence and what I call exfluence. Exfluence for me is a matter of borrowing or echoing one or more ideas, images, symbols or episodes. I would like to use the word influence, on the other hand, to indicate a sense of profound, penetrating, absorbing and pervasive impact on one's over-all attitude in life or on one's approach to the subject-matter. The way Eliot prefaces some of his poems with quotations from other poets and the way he echoes phrases, lines and passages from Shakespeare, Webster, Spenser, Dante, Marvell, Baudelaire, Ovid and others are examples of exfluence. The way some of the Romantic poets in Britain drew inspiration from the philosophical writings of Rousseau and Voltaire and the way the stream of consciousness novels like *Ulysses* were inspired by and were based on William James's concept of the unending and uneven flow of the mind are examples of what I would like to call influence. Similarly, the impact that Freud's concept of repressions, suppressions and inhibitions had on novels like *Women in Love* and *Lady Chatterly's Lover*, and on plays like *Mourning Becomes Electra* is another typical example of influence. De Witt Parker's book *The Analysis of Art* is a typical example of how a theory of art and literature can be influenced by a theory of psychology. The word "influence" is, as we know, the anglicized from of the Latin word *influentia*, the past participle form of a compound verb meaning "flow in". In the case of exfluence the effect flows on the surface and in mild trickles, whereas in the case of influence it flows in the form of an overpowering stream and sometimes even in the form of a deluge. Influence colours and determines the author's basic attitude and affects the texture of his emotive fibre. When one examines the possible impact of one theory of literature on another, one ought to be clear in one's mind, therefore, about this difference between exfluence and influence.

### 1.2 *Emotive and Fictive Universals*

Emotions like the emotion of love, hatred, sorrow and jealousy are basic human emotions of a global and universal nature: they transcend the limits of time, place and specific cultures. There is no ethnic community which has not got its own stories or poems about love between a man and a woman, about the beauty of nature, about the immense sorrow caused by the unexpected death of a lover or a beloved. Every community in history has distinguished between "the good" and "the evil" and every community has its real or legendary hero(es) who fought against the forces of evil. Similarly, every community has applied its mind and its imagination to the identification of the ultimate and enduring reality underlying the apparent flux of things. These archetypal emotions and attitudes have always been operative as emotive, experiential and attitudinal universals of literature all over the world. Similarly, there is no ethnic community or no culture in which perceptive and imaginative people have not used similes, metaphors, images, symbols, allegories, parables, hyperbole, personification and the like. These figures of speech have been characteristic of the way imaginative people all over the world have structured their emotive perception. They cut across geographical, ethnic and cultural boundaries and they show that we all share an innate tendency towards certain modes of hypersemanticized expression. The use of these figures in one literature does not show the exfluence or the influence of another literature; it only shows that just as there are emotive and attitudinal universals, there are fictive universals which people of poetic sensibility all over the world have used at different times. No ethnic community consciously learns the use of these devices from another community or culture; they are manifestations of inborn predilections, of global predispositions towards organizing and structuring experiences. These fictive universals include the use of elemental images like the image of water, fire, wind, and the sky and primordial images and archetypes like the image of the mother earth, the circle and the wise old man, images which Jung considers to be the manifestations of the collective unconscious of the human race.

### 1.3 *The Fallacy of Over-generalization*

When making a generalized observation on Indian poetics or on Graeco-Roman poetics, one must not ignore the fact that neither of these two bodies of knowledge is homogeneous and monolithic. It is possible to argue that in spite of their internal heterogeneity the theories of literature developed in ancient Greece and Rome have a typical Graeco-Roman aura about them and that, similarly, the Indian theories of poetics, in spite of their differences, have about them a typical Indianness which binds them together. The differences between the main approaches in each of these two traditions must not be ignored, however.

1.3.1 Let us first of all consider the heterogeneity of the Graeco-Roman tradition of rhetoric and poetics. The sophists in ancient Greece identified virtue with eloquence wheras Plato identified virtue with truth and knowledge. The sophists believed in the power of the word, the power of rhetorical devices to persuade people to the speaker's point of view. Plato, on the other hand, believed that one should speak "so far as possible, in a manner pleasing to the gods." With the help of their rhetoric, sophists like Corax and Tisias wanted to make old things new and new things old, the big little and little big. Plato, however, believed, as Indian sages did, that truth was the first and foremost pre-requisite of the art of speaking. Those who identified wisdom with eloquence got an attitudinal support from the myth of Orpheus, who was believed to have the power of taming savage men and beasts but those who identified wisdom with truth derived inspiration from philosophers like Socrates and Diogenes and believed that the validity, the profundity and the vitality of the truth could speak for themselves without the help of any rhetoric. This controversy between philosophers and rhetoricians, i.e., between dialecticians like Plato on the one hand and orators like Isocrates on the other, became so pronounced that Plato went to the extent of making that highly controversial remark that poets had no place in the ideal republic conceptualized by him.

Aristotle was Plato's student and later he also taught rhetoric in the Academy started by his teacher. However, in the controversy of dialecticians versus rhetoricians he sided with rhetoricians and not with dialecticians represented by his teacher, Plato. His teacher advocated the nobility and truthfulness of the content of what one had to say but in his opinion "speeches owe their effect not so much to the sense as to the style" (*Rhetoric* III.i). About style he said (*Rhetoric* III.i) that "it is not sufficient to know what one ought to say, — but one must know how to say it ...". He welcomed wisdom if it was eloquent but asserted, nevertheless, that "if it be inquired which is the more eminent excellence, I give the palm to the learned orator". He added further that "if you insist on distinguishing the orator from the philosopher, the philosopher will be inferior ...". We can say, therefore, as Wimsatt and Brooks (1964 : 68) have done, that Aristotle defended rhetoric on approximately the same grounds as those on which Plato condemned it.

In my opinion one of the great contributions of the Graeco-Roman tradition to the history of ideas about literature is the notion of the sublime. But I view this notion of the sublime enunciated by Longinus more as a protest against his predecessors' ideas about language and literature than as an affirmation of those ideas. Sophists like Corax and Tisias had reduced rhetoric to the low level of a utilitarian skill for someone to be able to defeat his opponent in a court of law or to excel him in eloquence on the occasion of a festival or to impress the audience with one's eloquence on the occasion of a funeral. Projecting the notion of literature characterized by the sublimity of passion was a befitting ideological protest against the sophist's view of the role that a figurative and hypersemanticised use of language ought to play in life. The distinction that Longinus makes between poetry and rhetoric in the first chapter of his book expresses his protest against the sophists' use of language for unimaginative purposes. He makes his views abundantly clear when he says that "the effect of elevated language upon an audience is not persuasion but transport". Longinus defined sublimity as the echo of a great soul and said that "it was not possible that men with mean and servile ideas ... should produce anything that is admirable and worthy of immortality". His concept of sublimity was also a protest against Plato's notion of a dialectician as opposed to a rhetorician. As Cicero (*De Oratore* III, 16) has rightly pointed out, Plato separated the ability to think wisely from the ability to speak eloquently and paid little attention to the role that eloquence ought to play in a philosopher's expression of his wisdom. Longinus defined sublimity as a dynamic togetherness of the following:

(i) the power of forming great conceptions
(ii) inspired and vehement passion
(iii) formation of figures
(iv) noble diction
(v) dignified and elevated composition

The first two of these constituents of sublimity as defined by Longinus can be taken to be a protest against the sophists' narrowly utilitarian view of the art of speaking and the remaining three can be taken to be a protest against Plato's view that a philosopher was to be known for his wisdom and not necessarily for his eloquence.

1.3.2 Just as Graeco-Roman rhetoric is not homogeneous and monolithic, Indian poetics is not homogeneous and monolithic either. Bharata, the earliest known proponent of the *rasa theory*, for example, was of the firm view that *rasa*, i.e., art emotion, was the vital essence of poetry. Ornamentation in the use of language was desirable only in so far as it was instrumental in evoking these art emotions. Bharata's emphasis, in other words, was on the emotive and imaginative content of poetry and not on its form. But Bhamaha shifted the emphasis from content to form and considered *alankaras*, i.e., ornamentation achieved through a figurative use of language, to be a defining feature of poetry. Poetry for Bhamaha was an over-semanticized linguistic act and *alankaras* were the typical device for achieving that over-semanticization. In Bhamaha's opinion, therefore, *alankaras* did not add to poetic beauty; they produced it. Bhamaha distinguished between *varta*, i.e., everyday use of language and *sahitya*, i.e., literature, and said that literature was characterized by a certain strikingness or charm absent in the day-to-day use of language. But those who aligned themselves with the *alankara* school later said a number of conflicting and contradictory things about alankara. Dandin, for example, was of the opinion that simplicity had its own beauty and grandeur and, therefore, he described *svabhavokti*, i.e., unadorned expressions, as the most ancient and the most primordial of all alankaras. Vamana and Jagannath made absolutely no mention of it as an alankara. Kuntaka went further and argued that it must not be considered an alankara at all.

In his exposition of the theory of *vakrokti*, Kuntaka also said more or less the same things as Bhamaha had said about the importance of alankara and described poetry as an attempt to transcend the dullness and ordinariness of the day-to-day use of language. For Kuntaka, as for Bhamaha, literature was an aesthetically appealing use of language capable of pleasing the connoisseur. So in spite of the small differences of details here and there Kuntaka's theory was a re-affirmation of the concept of poetry as form, of the view that poetry is not the thing said but a way of saying it. Thus even if we disregard the numerous other differences between the six main theories of literature in ancient India, we cannot ignore the fact that these theories fall in two distinct groups opposed to each other, one group represented by Bharata and his supporters like Anandavardhana, Bhanudatta and Bhattanayaka and the other one represented by Bhamaha, Kuntaka and others; one emphasizing the emotive and imaginative content of poetry and the other emphasizing the form. But though Kuntaka's theory of *vakrokti* is in many senses a re-affirmation of some of the basic tenets of Bhamaha's theory of *alankaras*, it is not just a re-statement, elaboration, enrichment or maturation of the theory propounded by Bhamaha; it is in many ways a refutation and a contradiction of some of Bhamaha's basic principles. Bhamaha, for example, described literature as a togetherness of word and meaning. Kuntaka repudiated this notion and said that not only literature but even non-literary uses of language are examples of togetherness of word and meaning. Literature, he said, was that togetherness of word and meaning which transcended the ordinariness of the day-to-day use of language and acquired an extraordinary charm and beauty. My aim here is not to provide an exhaustive list of conflicting views in Indian poetics but only to give a few illustrations in support of the fact that Indian poetics is not homogeneous and undirectional, each theorist only trying to re-affirm, validate, elaborate and illustrate his predecessor's views; it is a body of knowledge in which theorists have spent so much time refuting each other.

A Greek philosopher is reported to have said that nature has a liking for contraries and evolves harmony out of them and not out of similarities. It is difficult to say whether this principle of harmony evolving out of contrariety is true about the ontology of everything in nature but it certainly applies in a big way to Indian poetics and also to the rhetoric and poetics developed in ancient Greece and Rome. In a comparative study of Indian and Western poetics, it is necessary, therefore, to ensure that one does not make sweeping generalizations based on the mistaken assumption that each of these traditions is homogeneous and monolithic.

### 1.4 *Coincidental Parallels*

Besides, one must make a distinction between exfluence or influence on the one hand and coincidental parallels on the other. It would be naive to assume, for example, that if some of the statements made by Diogenes are strikingly similar to certain statements made by Buddha or Confucius, this necessarily means that at the time of making those statements Diogenes had a clear, prior knowledge of what Buddha, Confucius or Zarathustra had said and he was, therefore, only repeating his predecessor's views without acknowledging the source. If two men had similar or nearly identical dreams, it does not mean that one man's dream was "influenced" by that of the other. However, striking similarity may well be only a matter of chance coincidence and not a matter of exfluence or influence. This question of influence as opposed to chance coincidence becomes particularly important when we want to compare the theories of literature in India with those in ancient Greece and Rome. In the *Gita* (X. 37), for example, the word *kavi* has been used for a great sage (i.e., for Shukracharya), for a wise man (XVIII. 2) and also for God (VIII. 9). In *Kathopanishad* (I.iii.14) also this word has been used for a wise person. In Plato's *Ion*, as in the *Gita* and the *Kathopanishad*, the poet has been described as "a light and winged and holy thing". The *Gita* says (VII. 15) that austerity in the use of language consists in expressing oneself in such a way that it does not hurt and is pleasant, beneficial and supportive of truth. In a like manner, Plato emphasizes truth as the aim of speaking and in *Phaedrus* (260) he says that "a real art of speaking ... which does not seize hold of truth, does not exist and never will". In *Kathopanishad* (I.iii.3-9) there is an allegory in which the human body has been imagined to be a chariot, the intellect to be a charioteer, the senses to be the horses drawing that chariot and the mind to be a bridle. Likewise, in *Phaedrus* (244-245) Plato has used the allegory of a chariot in which the immortal soul or the intellective principle has been described as a charioteer driving with great difficulty his chariot with two horses, one of them being a noble horse personifying higher desire and the other one being a balky beast symbolizing lower passions. In Bhamaha's *Kavyalankar* (1.30,34; 2.87; 5.66) *vakrokti*, i.e., a clever remark or an oblique utterance has been described as the underlying principle of all figurative expressions and, therefore, the essence of poetry. Similarly, in *Rhetoric* (III.2 & 5), Aristotle argues in favour of a certain strangeness or departure from the ordinary which (like a foreigner among our fellow citizens) appears more distinguished. Like Aristotle and Bhamaha, Horace also considers such utterances to be a thing of vital importance and says the following:

> I will give a twist to the familiar that will make anybody think he could do the same—but he will waste his perspiration if he tries.
>
> *Ars Poetica* (240-242)

In his book *Auchitya Vichar Charcha* Kshemendra holds the view that propriety is the soul of poetry. In *Ars Poetica* (43) Horace holds a nearly identical view and argues in favour of the dictum of "a place for everything and everything in its place". Such striking similarities between Indian poetics and Graeco-Roman rhetoric can only be considered coincidental parallels; it would be naive to describe them in terms of exfluence or influence.

1.5 *The Chronological Evidence*

One of the dependable techniques for ascertaining whether the striking parallels between Indian and Graeco-Roman traditions of rhetoric and poetics are explanable in terms of exfluence and/or influence is to examine these two traditions of scholarship in a chronological perspective.

1.5.1 *The Probability of the Graeco-Roman Influence on Indian Poetics:* Indian poetics is believed to have its roots in the Vedas where the word *kavi* has been used as a synonym for *prophet* and *kavya* as a synonym for *prophetic art*. The word *rasa*, which names the central concept of the most widely acclaimed theory of Indian poetics, has been used in the *Rig Veda* in the sense of the sap or flavour of the honey of all things and as the essential property and virtue of the *rasvat* (RV VII.53.3; V.44.13; VI.47.1). The words *alankrit* and *alankriti* used in the *Rig Veda* (RV I.2.1, II.1.7 and VII.29.3) and the word *alankara* used in *Shatpatha Brahman* (XIII.8.4) anticipate the alankara school of Indian poetics formulated by Bhamaha. A systematic treatise of the principles of dramaturgy was not to be found anywhere in India until Bharata's book *Natyashastra* appeared. Many more theories of poetics were formulated in India later but this theory of poetics has always been estimated to be the most primordial theory and it has commanded the highest respect among intellectuals in India and abroad. The central point of this theory of *rasa*, i.e., art emotion, aroused by instinctual emotions like love, anger, hatred, and compassion. Though this theory was elaborated, elucidated and annotated by a number of theorists and commentators, the basic concepts of this theory as formulated by Bharata around the beginning of second century AD have always remained the same. Chronologically speaking, the second theory of poetics in India was the theory of *alankara* formulated by Bhamaha (700-750 AD). The third theory was the theory of *riti* (style), a theory which conceptualized *riti* as the soul of poetry. This theory was formulated sometime around the beginning of the ninth century. Anandvardhana's theory of *dhvani*, which postulated suggestiveness to be the vital essence of poetry, was presented in the book called *Dhvanyaloka*, which appeared in 902. Kuntaka's theory of *Vakrokti*, the theory which said that hypersemanticization was the crucial characteristic of literature and a figurative use of language was the device for achieving this hypersemanticization, became widely known sometime around the middle of the eleventh century. Although there is no definite information about when exactly Ksemendra's theory of *auchitya* (propriety) appeared in the form of his book *Auchitya Vichar Charcha*, his book is believed to have been written soon after 1050. This theory of propriety was thus the last original theory of poetics to be formulated in the tradition of Sanskrit poetics in India. Some scholarly books on Indian poetics were no doubt written even after the eleventh century. Ruyyaka (1150-1175), for example, wrote his book *Alankarsarvasva* in which, as a staunch supporter of the Dhvani school, he discussed the various figures of speech in Sanskrit. Similarly, Vishwanath (1300-1380) in his famous book *Sahityadarpana* discussed various aspects of poetry with special emphasis on Bharata's concept of *rasa*. The last book in this tradition was written by Jagannath (1620-1665). Jagannath was a man of professorial genius of wide reading and admirable critical understanding of the whole tradition of Indian poetics. He formulated no original theory of his own but showed, nevertheless, a scholarly understanding of all the schools of poetics in India. He provided his own definition of the concepts in Indian poetics and gave his own illustrations in support of those definitions. A profound scholar with a perceptive understanding of all different schools, he presented the information about Indian poetics in an eclectic manner. He was, however, the last Sanskrit rhetorician in India. Like a river that starts in the form of glaciers rolling down a snow-capped mountain, passes through various gorges, valleys, lakes and lagoons and ultimately gets lost in a desert with its endless sand dunes, the stream of Indian poetics that originated from the *Rig Veda*, derived its strength from the Upanishads and then the epics, disappeared for ever towards the end of the seventeenth century.

If we consider these facts in the perspective of the history of the use of English in India, we will find that the last great book in the history of Sanskrit poetics had already been written before Indians started learning English as a vehicle of art, philosophy and literature. It was on 31st December 1600 that Queen Elizabeth gave to the East India Company the charter of the monopoly of trade with India. Some traders, sailors, adventurers or missionaries may have visited India earlier than that charter but after that charter Englishmen started coming to India in organized groups and so people in India needed English to be able to communicate with them as these Englishmen needed Indian languages to be able to communicate with Indians. But even after that charter there was no organised teaching of English in India for a long time. In the eighteenth century Raghunath Hari Navalkar, the Governor of Jhansi under the Maharashtrian Ruler, the Sindhia of Gwalior, was perhaps one of the first to learn English in India but as there was no systematic and institutionalized teaching of English in India at that time, "he himself began to study English" with the purpose of learning physics and chemistry

(Chatterji 1978: 169). It was in 1766 that an educated Indian visited England for the first time but he was a Muslim scholar of Persian and Arabic (ibid) with no interest in Sanskrit poetics. It was as late as 1857 that the three Presidency colleges were started, one each in Bombay, Madras and Calcutta where arts and humanities were taught through the medium of English. The English language was for Indians the only window on the Graeco-Roman wisdom, particularly to the rhetoric and poetics that flourished in that tradition. But as has been pointed out earlier, the last theory of poetics in India had already been formulated by the middle of the eleventh century and the last great eclectic exposition of a scholastic type was also completed around the middle of the seventeenth century. As the teaching of English in India started only around the middle of the nineteenth century, it is not at all likely that when formulating their theories or even when annotating, elaborating, illustrating and supplementing the ideas of their predecessors or their contemporaries, Indian rhetoricians and aesthetes were under the exfluence or influence of the Graeco-Roman tradition of rhetoric and poetics.

1.5.2 *The Probability of the Indian Influence on Graeco-Roman Rhetoric and Poetics:* Just as the roots of Indian poetics can be traced back to the Vedas, Graeco-Roman poetics has its roots in Homer, who enunciated the principle of inspiration (*Iliad* II, 484-493) and differentiated between two styles of oratory (*Iliad* III, 203-224). It has its roots also in the rhetorical devices developed by the sophists, who in the ancient city states of Greece, taught people how to defend themselves or their friends and relatives against possible accusations. But deliberate, theoretical criticism began in Greece much later, with Aristophanes, Socrates and Plato. It was in its full blossom in the writings of Aristotle, Quintilian, Horace and Longinus. Aristophanes was basically a dramatist and not a theorizer or a practicing critic and his ideas about literature were expressed in the form of dialogues and episodes in his comedies like *Frogs*. Plato, who was a pupil and devoted admirer of Socrates, discussed literature at the level of philosophical abstractions. In his *Dialogues* in many of which Socrates figured as conducting the discussions, he discussed ideas of great importance about some of the basics of literature. He discussed, for example, his concept of beauty, his ideas about structure of a discourse and his contention that we must divide things only "where the natural joints are, and not trying to break any part after the manner of a bad carver". Plato died in 348 BC. Aristotle, who delineated the concept of catharsis as the soul of tragedy and can rightfully be considered to be one of the great pillars of literary theory in the West died in 322 BC. Horace and Quintilian, the two great figures in the history of literary theorizing in ancient Rome, died in 8 BC and around the end of the first century AD respectively. Longinus, the author of the book, *On the Sublime*, and the last great theorist in the ancient Graeco-Roman tradition is believed to have died some time in the third century AD. We can say, therefore, that the great books on poetics in the ancient Graeco-Roman tradition had all been written by the end of the third century AD after which the flame of ambitious originality in that intellectual domain started tapering off and finally got extinguished.

If we trace the history of Indo-Greek relations from the point of view of the exchange of ideas between the philosophers, mystics and rhetoricians of the two countries, we will find that the earliest known contact between the two countries was established at the time of the Greek invasion on India. This invasion took place in 329 BC and Alexander left India in 325 BC. The University of Taxila was at the height of its fame and glory at that time and "was known to all Asia as the leading seat of Hindu scholarship, renowned above all for its medical school". We are told that students "flocked to Taxila as in the middle ages they flocked to Paris; there all arts and sciences could be studied under eminent professors, and the medical school especially was held in high repute throughout the oriental world". This statement makes it clear that the University of Taxila had students from all over the oriental world but it is not abundantly clear whether it had students from Greece as well. Even if it is established that this university had students from Greece also, it is not certain whether it had students from that country to study poetics in India. Besides, if the speculations regarding the date of composition of the *Natyashastra* are to be believed, it was written sometime during the second, third or fourth century AD. It is quite likely that by the time the *Natyashastra* became established as good enough to be used as a textbook for the teaching of dramaturgy, the university of Taxila had started declining, with few students, if any at all, coming from countries like Greece.

Megasthenese came to Pataliputra in 300 BC as the ambassador of the Syrian King Seleucus Nicator and stayed in India until 298 BC. There is no dependable historical evidence for us to be able to say that there ever was at least an occasional, if not a regular, exchange of scholars between India and Greece before Megasthenese came to India as an ambassador. Megasthenese took back to Greece a great deal of information about Indian manners, customs and laws and also about the system of government and education in India. But he was not a man of literature and there is no evidence to suggest that when leaving India he took with him either the original or the translation of anything on Indian poetics. Besides, if the *Natyashastra* is the first book of poetics in the Indian tradition and if it is true that this book was not written earlier than the second century AD, then there was no book on poetics that Megasthenese could have taken with himself. The University of Nalanda was another seat of learning in ancient India. It is believed to have started soon after the death of the Buddha. It is not at all likely that students from Greece or Rome studied Indian poetics at the University of Nalanda because from the very beginning this university was a centre of learning for Buddhist studies and Indian poetics has largely been a Hindu discipline deriving its inspiration from Hindu scriptures like the *Vedas* and the *Upanishads* and not from any one of the Buddhist scriptures. It was towards the end of the eighteenth century that Indological studies became a fascinating subject for Western scholars. Charles Wilkins' translation of the *Gita* was published in 1785, William Jones' translation of Kalidasa's *Shakuntala* was published in 1789 and Colebrooke's essays on the *Vedas* were published in 1809. Anquitil Duperron's translation of a Persian translation of the *Upanishads* was published about the same time. Maxmuller's books were all published years later during the nineteenth century. It can be safely assumed, therefore, that until about the middle of the nineteenth century Greek scholars were not familiar with any one of the schools of Indian poetics. As the outflow of information about Indian classics to European countries started only around the middle of the nineteenth century, it is not very likely that any one of the great books on rhetoric or poetics written in ancient Greece or Rome was ever influenced by theories of Indian poetics or that it had on it even a casual exfluence of any one of the theories of Indian poetics.

In view of all this, research workers doing a comparative study of Indian and Graeco-Roman poetics need to be very cautious when making observations on the similarities between the two traditions. It may be tempting for them to conclude that the similarities between the two traditions show the influence of one on the other but a closer investigation will show that these similarities are examples of coincidental parallels and not results of influence or even of exfluence.

I would like to emphasize here, nevertheless, that, like most other things to be done only with caution, only a comparative study of these two immensely rich traditions of literary theories is something really worth doing. Very little is known until now about the similarities and the differences between Indian poetics and its Graeco-Roman counterpart but as research progresses, more and more will, hopefully, be known about how great minds in these two cultures completely independent and isolated from each other have theorized about the emotive and imaginative universe of literature. Literature depicts realities operating at a much deeper level of awareness than the mundane trivialities to be found on the surface of our day-to-day existence. Poetics is concerned with what this deeper, imaginative level of awareness is like and how the spirit of that imaginative awareness can best be captured in words. Thus, the study of poetics takes us to the emotive and imaginative roots of the culture in which it was formulated. Greece and Rome are places which nurtured and nourished one of the most glorious cultures in human history and, similarly, India is the ancient seat of another culture known for its glorious achievements. A comparative study of the theories of poetics developed in these two ancient seats of culture will take us, therefore, to the emotive and imaginative roots of mankind in these two ancient cultures and thereby enhance our understanding of ourselves.

A very unfortunate thing about scholars in India is that very few of them have the expertise necessary for studies involving a comparison of Indian poetics with its Graeco-Roman counterpart. There are scholars who have a profound knowledge of the critical tradition in the West but most of them virtually know nothing about Indian poetics. Similarly, there are Sanskrit scholars who have a superb knowledge and understanding of Indian poetics but they have no knowledge at all of what Aristotle, Horace, Longinus and others had to say about literature. Most Sanskrit scholars in India consider Graeco-Roman poetics to be something alien to their sensibility. Because of their isolation from the Western theories of literature, many of them develop an inflated sense of pride and start believing that no Western theory of literature can ever prove equal to Sanskrit poetics from the point of view of its subtlety and its comprehensiveness. In a like manner most scholars of English literature consider Sanskrit poetics to be obscurantist, old-fashioned and esoteric. There is in India, therefore, a dearth of scholars with the aptitude, the scholarship and above all the academic courage and confidence necessary for a comparative study of Indian poetics and its Graeco-Roman counterpart. Dr R P Sharma's scrutiny of *rasa* and catharsis and, similarly, his scrutiny of *auchitya* and decorum in this book, therefore, are investigations done in an area where there is and has always been a great need for such investigations. He makes no sweeping generalizations and does not start a futile and obsessive search for influence. His papers on Sanskrit and Graeco-Roman poetics show a profound critical awareness of the two traditions and I consider these papers to be a very valuable contribution to knowledge.

II

**2. Psychoanalysis and Theories of Literature**

2.1 *Need for Circumspection*

This book starts with a comparative study of Sanskrit poetics and its Graeco-Roman counterpart and then moves to the area of psychoanalysis, another area of great interest to poetics. The contribution of psychoanalysis to poetics has always been a matter of great controversy. The moment one thinks about psychoanalysis, one inevitably thinks about his concept of sexuality and his concept of repression and neurosis. Freud's theory of psychoanalysis is of such a radical and daring nature that it tends to provoke either an enthusiastic and uncritical support characteristic of religious fanaticism or a downright condemnation of something morbid, something sacrilegious. Wollheim (1971: 9), for example, thinks that it "would be hard to find in the history of ideas, even in the history of religion, someone whose influence was so immediate, so broad and so deep". Freud was of the view that the libido, the prime psychic force, was nothing but sexual energy and that all human behaviour was ultimately motivated by sexuality. As a consequence of that Freudian view of sex, some of his enthusiastic supporters have exaggerated the importance of sex beyond all proportions. Bonaparte (1949: 294), for example, is of the view that "almost all symbolism is sexual ... from the cradle to the grave". Some enthusiastic supporters of his theory of sexuality believe that images of objects that are concave in shape, e.g., images of cups, vases, hollows, caves, ponds and even flowers are all symbols of the female genital organ or of the womb and, similarly, images of things in the case of which length exceeds the diameter, e.g., images of snakes, knives, lenses, swords, peaks, towers and mountains are all phallic symbols (See Guerin et al 1979: 128). Critics like Desmond McCarthy on the other hand hold the view that the intrusion of psychoanalysis into the field of criticism "nearly always makes for stupidity" (Quoted in K Ahmad's book *Psychoanalysis and Literary Criticism*, p 5). In McCarthy's view psychoanalysts "notice certain tendencies in famous authors akin to those they have studied in the insane and clap asylum names upon them". "The medical minded critic", McCarthy adds further, "writes as though the finest genius might as well be in the clinic instead of outside it. He sees what an artist has in common with madness—and nothing else". There are scholars no doubt who have taken an objective, impartial and balanced view, those who have spoken highly of the praiseworthy aspects of Freud's theory but have at the same time criticized its inadequacies. We need more and more of such balanced scholars with a highly developed sense of fact so that the world of ideas about poetics is dominated not by fierce emotion but by reason and circumspection. A researcher attempting to evaluate Freud's contribution to knowledge has to keep reminding himself of the dictum that a theory has to establish itself on grounds of the proveness of its premise, its evidence, its arguments and its conclusions; it cannot be accepted or rejected simply because it sounds shockingly daring and original.

One of the main reasons for the accumulating confusion and misunderstanding in this area has been a great dearth of scholars with capabilities required for interdisciplinary studies and research. As Guerin et al (1979: 122) have rightly pointed out, "many critics of the psychological school have been either literary scholars who have understood the principles of psychology imperfectly or professional psychologists who have had little feeling for literature as art. The former have abused Freudian insights through oversimplification and distortion; the latter have bruised our literary sensibilities". Scholars wanting to apply Freud's principles to a work of art need to have not only a mature understanding of Freud's principles but also the perceptivity required for a proper appreciation of the aesthetic qualities of a work of art.

### 2.2 *Freud's Theory in Relation to the Past*

Freud's concept of sexuality is an extremely vital part of his theory of psychoanalysis, so vital that in the minds of many of his admirers the name of the master has become more or less synonymous with the notion of sexuality. But in spite of the fact that this concept occupies a central place of importance in his theory, it would be naive to equate this part with the whole of his theory. Certain other aspects of his theory, though not equally radical in their focus, deserve no less attention. One of such important aspects of his theory is his tripartite division of the human mind into the id, the ego and the super ego. This division is particularly important for a proper understanding of how conflicting tendencies, i.e., the id and the ego pull us in opposite directions and how the third psychic force, i.e., the super ego, reconciles these two conflicting trends. In Freud's view the id is a lawless, asocial, amoral, inaccessible and amorphous source of energy and vitality.To quote Freud's own words, it is "a chaos, a cauldron of seething excitement [with] no organisation and no unified will, only an impulsion to obtain satisfaction for the instinctual needs" (Freud 1964: 104-105). The ego is that aspect of the psyche which governs and regulates the instinctual drives of the id and exercises rational control over it. In Freud's opinion, "the ego stands for reason and circumspection, while the id stands for the untamed passions". The super ego is the repository of conscience and pride. It is "the representative of all moral restrictions, the advocate of the impulse toward perfection, in short it is as much as we have been able to apprehend psychologically of what people call the `higher' things in life" (p 95).

It seems to me that Freud's notion of the id can be interpreted in more than one way. It can, for example, be interpreted as the evil forces driving man towards destruction. Guerin et al (1979: 125) interpret his notion of the id in this manner and say that "the id as defined by Freud is identical in many respects to the Devil as defined by theologians". This identification of the id with the forces of evil inside man reminds us of Plato's concept of "the wild beast in our nature... which when men are asleep starts up and walks about naked, ... there is no conceivable folly or crime ... of which such a nature may not be guilty - not excepting incest or parricide" (K Ahmad's *Psychoanalysis*, p 2). This interpretation of the id and its relationship with the ego and the superego sounds like a restatement in a modern idiom of Plato's allegory (*Phaedrus*, pp 244-245) of a chariot in which the soul has been described as the charioteer, one of the two horses as a symbol of untamed passions for downward things in life. Another possible interpretation, and perhaps the better one, is to take the id as uncontrolled energy and not as something necessarily devilish. This interpretation will be compatible with Freud's view that the id is only "amoral" and not devilish in the sense of being anti-moral and that it "knows no values, no good and evil, no morality" (p 105). As Freud considers the id to be amoral and not anti-moral, it would be a distortion to interpret it as an evil force, as Guerin et al have done. It seems to me that Freud's tripartite division of the psychic energy into three zones has a striking resemblance to the image of the chariot in the *Gita* where the horses can be described as symbols of amoral and untamed passions and as a primordial source of all psychic energy, Arjuna as the symbol of "reason and circumspection" and Lord Krishna as the symbol of "the impulse toward perfection" and of "what people call the higher things in human life".

I would like to emphasize here, nevertheless, that it is not important whether Freud's tripartite division of the human psyche takes us closer to Plato's allegory or to the allegory of the chariot in the *Gita;* the important thing is to note that although Freud's notion of sexuality as the primordial source of energy seems to be something utterly original, there are other aspects of his theory which remind us of certain archetypal images used in ancient India and also in ancient Greece. We can argue, therefore, that although Freud's notion of sexuality as the motivation behind everything we do in life is shockingly new, there is still a point in examining his theory in the perspective of the history of ideas in Europe. One of the admirable qualities of Dr Sharma's book on poetics is that it examines Freud's theory not in isolation but in relation to relevant currents and cross-currents of ideas in the past and goes to the extent of quoting extracts from the *Gita* and the *Manusmriti,* which seem apparently to have no links with Freud's theory at all.

2.3 *Jung as Freud's Ideological Adversary*

Just as Aristotle, Plato's student, turned out to be Plato's strong ideological opponent, Adler, Freud's student, proved to be one of the powerful opponents of Freud's theory of psychoanalysis based on the notion of sexuality. Adler argued that the primary drive in life was not the instinct for sexuality but the instinct for power. For Adler, the fundamental law of life was the law of striving for power, for domination, for superiority over others; and literature, therefore, could best be understood as a manifestation of that drive for superiority. Adler's view of superiority had a striking parallel in Nietzsche's view that "all that increases the feeling of power, the will to power, power itself in man" is good and that "all that comes from weakness" is bad (Durant 1953: 426). It can well be imagined that Adler's theory, like Nietzsche's, had a great deal of appeal for leaders like Hitler and Musolini and for power-hungry politicians all over the world but it had very little impact on literary theory or literary criticism. For many people, Adler had only replaced one form of obsession by another. The psychoanalyst whose principles were widely accepted was Jung. Freud's theory of sexuality had successfully created a sense of confusion, a sense of bewilderment, a sense of shock and spiritual agony. People in India, as in many other countries of the world, had believed all their lives that mothers were to be worshipped like goddesses and in one of the Semitic religions it was said that heaven was located beneath the feet of one's mother, but then Freud interpreted one's love for the mother as an unconscious incestuous desire for the fulfilment of sexuality. Flowers have since time immemorial been considered to be a thing of beauty but Freud's theory said that, like other oval objects, flowers were symbols of the female genital organ just as swords, lances, spears and the like were symbols of the male genital organ and not of heroism and chivalry. Shelley had defined poetry as "the record of the best and happiest moments of the happiest and best minds" but for Freud poetry was a form of neurosis. Because of all this, people all over the world, those who believed in spiritual values, keenly felt the need for another psychoanalyst who could rescue them from the sense of shame and spiritual agony created by Freud's theory of sexuality. In place of terms like *anal eroticism, phallic symbol, Oedipus complex, genital primacy,* the world now needed elevating ideas and symbols which could inspire confidence in man's dignity once again. Jung's theory fulfilled that great spiritual need of the age. Like the first refreshing shower in a tropical country in summer and like a cool and soothing breeze coming from a snow-capped mountain to people getting restless in the scorching heat of a desert, Jung's theory of psychoanalysis came as a great solace. Jung restored the dignity of man. Freud had silenced and bewildered the world with what he called evidence. Like Freud, Jung, too, was a medical practitioner, a psychotherapist; and like Freud he based his conclusions on empirical data interpreted inductively. But Jung did something that Freud had not done. He interpreted his data not in isolation; he interpreted it in the larger perspective of what some of the best minds of the world, poets, philosophers and scientists, for example, had said in the best moments of their introspection. He condemned Freud's theory as a theory of psychology without any psyche in it. He restored the spirit back to its place of ancient glory and said that "it is easy to drive the spirit out of the door but, when we have done so the salt of life grows flat — it loses its savour" (Jung 1933: 142). He further added that "the wheel of history must not be turned back, and man's advance toward a spiritual life, which began with the primitive rites of initiation, must not be denied." (p 141) He reaffirmed the craving of the inner spirit and said,

> The current flows backward to its source; the inner man wants something which the visible man does not want, and we are at war with ourselves (p 233).

He proved on the basis of the numerous patients examined by him that although some cases of neurosis were genuine cases of the repression of the instinct for sexual gratification, the vast majority of such cases were cases of spiritual stagnation and psychic sterility. "A psycho-neurosis must be understood", he said, "as the suffering of a human being who has not discovered what life means for him". About the neurotic patients that he had examined, he said,

> Among all my patients in the second half of life—that is to say over thirty-five, there has not been one whose problem in the last resort was not that of finding a religious outlook on life. It is safe to say that every one of them fell ill because he had lost that which the living religions of every age have given to their followers, and none of them has been really healed who did not regain his religious outlook (p 264).

For him religions were "systems for healing psychic illness" (p 278) and so psychotherapists must occupy themselves with "problems which, strictly speaking, belong to the theologian."

Freud had postulated the existence of instincts and now

Jung argued in favour of the spirit and said that the existence of the spirit was no less certain than that of instincts.

> I do not doubt that the natural instincts or drives are forces of propulsion in human life, whether we call them sexuality or the will to power; but I also do not doubt that these instincts come into collision with the spirit, for they are continually colliding with something, and why should not this something be called spirit? (p 136)

He was aware of the fact that it was difficult to provide an exact definition of the spirit but he considered that to be no serious disadvantage because it was not possible to define the instinct either.

> I am far from knowing what spirit is in itself, and equally far from knowing what instincts are. The one is as mysterious to me as the other. (ibid)

Freud's concept of the dominating and overwhelming influence of the sexual drive on everything in life was a big ideological blow to the values that the East had always prized very high. Under the devastating influence of Freud's theory, many of the ideas which constituted the emotional citadel of the East seemed to crumble like a house of cards. People in the East had, for example, considered fathers to be persons worthy of great respect but Freud's theory forced them to believe that every boy had an unconscious rivalry with his father for the love of his mother. Jung reversed the attitudinal focus of his theory of psychoanalysis and glorified the East.

> ... we do not yet realize that while we are turning upside down the material world of the East with our technical proficiency, the East with its psychic proficiency is throwing our spiritual world into confusion. We have never yet hit upon the thought that while we are overpowering the Orient from without, it may be fastening its hold upon us from within. (p 249)

For Jung, images and symbols were not an oblique fulfilment of the suppressed instinct for sexuality in the personal life of the poet; they were expressions of the collective unconscious of the whole human race. The primordial images used by poets were "older than historical man" and "ingrained in him from earliest times, and, eternally living, outlasting all generations". He held the view that "it is possible to live the fullest life only when we are in harmony with these symbols; wisdom is a return to them." (p 130)

Poets like Shelley were of the view that poetry "redeems from decay the visitations of the divinity in man." (cited Wimsatt and Brooks, p 420) and that poets were "the mirrors of the gigantic shadows which futurity casts upon the present." Freud brought poets down from that high pedestal and described them as pathological cases of psycho-neurosis. Jung raised the status of poets once again and said that they had the ability to draw upon "the healing and redeeming forces of the collective psyche" and to penetrate to "that matrix of life in which all men are embedded, which imparts a common rhythm to all human existence, and allows the individual to communicate his feeling and his striving to mankind as a whole (p 198).

Thus, Jung's theory was in many ways a reverse image of Freud's theory. So, if Dr Sharma had written a paper only on Freud or only on Jung, the book would have presented a fragmentary and disproportionate picture of psychoanalysts' views on poetics. The two papers taken together present a comprehensive critical survey of what psychoanalysts have to say about the basic problems and principles in poetics.

When reading this book one cannot but be impressed by the author's perceptivity, his highly developed sense of fact and his superb analytical ability, and, therefore, I introduce this book to the reader with a sense of great pride and pleasure.

*Sana'a University, Sana'a* **D Thakur**
*Republic of Yemen*
*5 June 1996*

# Rasa and Catharsis: Intersecting Theories of Aesthetic Pleasure

No comparison between the *Natyashastra* and the *Poetics* can possibly override the natural and numerous differences between them. No one will possibly deny that differences between these classics (as between any two great works or authors) arise from a number of obvious factors. Some of these factors are language, time, place and culture. But a comparison becomes an interesting exercise mainly because the works are different and it is the *distance* between the works that provides the motivation for the attempt to bring out similarities between them.

One of the aims of this study is to point out that many areas of broad similarity between the *Natyashastra* and the *Poetics* can be convincingly identified and discussed. However, the main purpose of this article is to focus attention on some of the important and easily identifiable threads of similarity between the theory of Rasa and the theory of Catharsis. It will be argued that the two theories (provided we keep in mind the fundamental difference between the Indian and Greek traditions of drama) seem to be nearly alternative formulations of what is usually called "aesthetic pleasure". But, before the similarities are discussed, it is important to offer a few clarifications.

First, it must be pointed out that this discussion of similarities between the *Natyashastra* and the *Poetics* does not presume any borrowing or influence between the two works. Keith's arrogant conclusion that the independent development of Bharata's theory of drama is "as probable as borrowing" (1924: 356) is both unwarranted and untenable, as it is supercilious to known history and to convincing logic. Keith's conclusion is one of those off-the-cuff remarks which are seldom based on facts or arguments. Nowhere in his book does one find an argument to support the generalization that the *Natyashastra* may have been influenced by the *Poetics*. Keith seems to have drawn his conclusion from a very simple, almost naive and premise. He found certain parallels of Aristotle's theory of drama in the *Natyashastra* and therefore concluded that it must have been borrowed from the Greek original.

Keith's conclusion, we must note, is not supported by the facts of known history. The *Poetics* is generally believed to be one of the last works of Aristotle (cf Dorsch 1965: 15, Golden and Hardison 1968: 56, Mckeon 1957, Roberts 1946: V) and may have been written anytime between 335 and 322 BC. But in the case of the *Natyashastra*, several probable dates of its composition have been suggested. These dates vary from the fifth century BC to the fourth century AD (cf Keith 1924: 291—towards the close of fourth century AD, Kane 1971 : 47—not later then AD 300, De 1960: 18—second century BC to second century AD, Dalal 1973: 38—BC 200/300, Shastri 1973: 93—fifth century BC). In view of this controversy, it is not proper to affirm that the *Natyashastra* — either followed or preceded the *Poetics*. Apart from this, there is no other plausible basis to say that the *Natyashastra* was influenced by the *Poetics*. There seems to have been no linguistic or literary exchange between India and Greece in those days. The political contacts between these countries dating back to the last quarter of the fourth century BC (cf McGraw-Hill, 1973, Vol I: 124 & Vol II: 473-74) do not prove any exchange of literary scholarship. As far as is generally known, it was only towards the end of the eighteenth century that Sir William Jones pioneered a movement, as it were, for the exchange of ideas on language and literature between India and the West. Jones' *discovery* of Sanskrit became known to the West only after he had made the famous pronouncement at the meeting of the Royal Asiatic Society in Calcutta (1786) that "Sanskrit is of a wonderful structure, more perfect than the Greek, more copious than the Latin, and more exquisitely refined than either" (quoted in Robins 1967: 134).

Besides, there is no evidence to suggest that Bharata knew Greek or that Sanskrit translations of the *Poetics* were made available to him. The view, therefore, taken in this article is that both Bharata (fifth century BC ?) and Aristotle (384-322 BC) developed their respective theories of drama independently and that there is no borrowing on either side.

The second clarification concerns the use of Aristotle's *tragedy* and Bharata's *drama* as almost interchangeable terms for the purpose of the present discussion. Quite obviously, Aristotle's use of the term *tragedy* is in consonance with the contemporary Greek usage. The Greeks, as we all know, did not insist on an equation between tragedy and a story with an unhappy ending (cf Dorius 1980). Sophocles and Euripides, for instance, wrote tragedies with a happy ending, i.e., the *philoctetes* (Sophocles), *Alcestis* and *Iphigenia in Tauris* (both by Euripides). Etymologically, tragedy means a *goat song* which could refer to the prize of the winner (a goat), or to the dress (goat-skin) of performers, or to the sacrificial goat (cf Conversi 1980). In ancient Greece tragedy was used as a label for any one of the three plays performed at a dramatic festival. On each day of a dramatic festival, four plays were performed, three generally serious in tone and one satyr play. Tragedy, thus, meant a serious play. Aristotle's definition of tragedy, therefore, needs to be interpreted in this context. Many of the plays that Aristotle refers to as tragedies could, in fact, be "considered romances or even comedies by modern standards, as, for example, *Oedipus at Colonus* and the *Eumenides*" (Golden & Hardison 1968: 113). Additionally, it is interesting to note that of the thirty and odd tragedies mentioned in the *Poetics* the two most frequently cited for illustration of his theoretical observations are *Oedipus Rex* and *Iphigenia in Tauris*. The two ideal plots of tragedy, according to Aristotle, are, the complex fatal plot and the complex-fortunate plot (cf Golden & Hardison 1968: 166). Reversal (peripety) and recognition or discovery (anagnorisis) are those factors of a tragedy which distinguish a complex plot from a simple one (cf *Poetics* VI: 73-75, XXI: 3-6). That a tragedy must have a complex fatal plot is taken for granted but the assumption that a play which has a complex fortunate plot is also a tragedy (and that too as good as the other one) creates problems for modern commentators on the *Poetics*. The doctrine of a complex fortunate plot as one of the two ideal plots of tragedy is supported by what Aristotle says at several places in the *Poetics*. In chapter VII (lines 43-45) he talks about a change of fortune from *bad to good*. Similarly in chapter XI he mentions both *Oedipus* and *Iphigenia* to illustrate his notion of the best complex plot in which recognition occurs together with reversal. Discussing the possible combinations of recognition and the tragic deed in chapter XIV, he claims that the *most effective type* is the one in which the recognition precedes the act (sic) so that the tragic act is averted as in "the *Cresphontes*, where Merope is going to kill her son and does not, but on the contrary, recognizes him, and in the *Iphigenia*, where a sister is involved in a similar situation with a brother, and in the *Helle*, where a son is about to surrender his mother recognizes her" (XIV: 63-68). Again, in chapter XVII he mentions *Iphigenia* in connection with his discussion of the *appropriate episodes* for a tragic plot. As recognition is a "change from ignorance to knowledge", it evokes *pity and fear* and is capable of giving *happiness and misery* (cf XI: 11,22 X: 23).

A careful examination of the *Poetics* would reveal that the two indispensable ingredients of tragedy are: (i) misfortune (i.e. the nexus of fearful and pitiable incidents) and (ii) a combination of recognition and reversal. But the dividing line between a fatal and a fortunate tragedy is drawn by the temporal sequence of recognition and the tragic act. Aristotle defines reversal as the change of fortune in the action of the play to "the opposite state of affairs" (XI: 1-2). Necessarily related to recognition, reversal occurs in every tragedy. But whether a tragedy is going to be fortunate or fatal depends on whether the change from ignorance to knowledge (i.e. recognition) takes place before or after the tragic act. In the Aristotelian scheme it is not crucial whether a tragedy is going to have a happy or miserable ending; that which really makes a tragedy, a tragedy is the presence of misfortune which is another term for tragic conflict. The presence of conflict or misfortune is crucial to a tragedy. Now, since Aristotle does not insist on a necessary correlation between a tragedy and an unhappy ending of the plot, the term *tragedy* acquires a much broader connotation than its present day usage would suggest. Taken in this broad Aristotelian sense where it is almost interchangeable with `serious play', tragedy is seen in the present study as a term which shares a semantic fraternity with Bharata's use of *drama*. Once again, we must keep in mind the fundamental distance between tragedy and drama as used by Aristotle and Bharata respectively. The semantic fraternity between these terms must, therefore, be seen as restricted to the extent to which they refer to serious plays.

The commonplace distinction between tragedy and drama is sought to be blurred in this article also from another point of view. As in the *Natyashastra*, quite a few of the theoretical constructs used in the *Poetics* in relation to tragedy could equally effectively be applied to the analysis of drama, perhaps, even to that of literature in general. Aristotle himself blurs the distinction between poetry and tragedy (cf Wimsatt and Brooks 1964: 35) as Bharata does in relation to the distinction between *Kavya* (poetry) and *Natya* (drama) (cf Kane 1971: 355). Tragedy is treated in the *Poetics* as the most representative form of literature and the author believes that "whoever can judge what is good and bad in tragedy can do this in regard to epic" (V: 34-35), and one might add, perhaps also in regard to the other genres of literature.

The third and final clarification that needs to made here is the one that relates to a popular misconception about the historical estimate of the *Poetics*. The *Poetics*, we must remember, is an independent and self-contained work, a positive analysis. It must not be rated as a defence of poetry or as a refutation of Plato's animadversions to poetry. That certain parts of the *Poetics* turn out to be a refutation of Plato's argument against poetry and poets may well be considered incidental to the over-all structure and argument of this work. It is a fact that Aristotle held views about poetry which were different from or contrary to those which Plato held. But this need not lead to the conclusion that Aristotle wrote his treatise on the science of Poetics only to refute what his illustrious teacher had said. The *Poetics* performed a much loftier function than a mere refutation. It was, in fact, the earliest attempt in the Western tradition to establish the study of Poetry as a discipline in itself—a discipline as responsible and respectable as any other. This shift in the basic emphasis of the attitude to the *Poetics* has a crucial bearing on the remaining part of this write-up.

Rene Wellek and Austin Warren in their book *The Theory of Literature* distinguish between *literary theory* and *literary criticism* by defining the former as "the study of the principles of literature, its categories, criteria, and the like" and the latter as the study of *concrete works* of literature (1963: 49). With this distinction in mind we can describe the *Poetics* and the *Natyashastra* as studies in literary theory. Neither of them is an empirical study of specific works of literature. They are universally regarded as the earliest and the most comprehensive treatises on the theory of drama that have survived through the ages. The *Poetics*, like the *Natyashastra*, is essentially the poetics of the drama. Full of condensed and aphoristic statements, both of these works are complex and difficult documents. Some of their maxims have the shape of algebraic formulas. Each of these books is an acroamatic text, that is, a text which cannot be fully explicated without the help of other texts.

Many of the similarities between the *Poetics* and the *Natyashastra* seem to emanate not only from the fact that they deal with the same subject matter, but also from their following an almost identical frame of reference. They build their generalizations about the theory of drama on the basis of this frame of reference. The four coordinates that constitute this frame of reference may be called matter, means, manner and function. Aristotle's definition of tragedy illustrates these four coordinates of dramatic theory (*Poetics* VI: 4-11). Similarly, Bharata speaks of the four components of drama in chapter I of the *Natyashastra* (verse 17). Aristotle's exposition uses terms like 'imitation', 'language', 'presentation', and 'catharsis' while Bharata's description mentions terms like *pathya* (text), *geet* (song), *abhinaya* (presentation) and *Rasa* (aesthetic pleasure). The difference in their respective terminologies is not very important. The striking similarity between the two approaches is evident from each of them using a theoretical framework consisting of four parts. As is so well known, Aristotle believed that four causes cooperate to produce a phenomenon, whether natural or artificial. These four causes are: the material cause, the formal cause, the efficient cause, and the final cause. The four coordinates of the dramatic theory presented in the *Natyashastra* (as in the *Poetics*) are comparable to the four Aristotelian causes. The present write-up seeks to discuss the parallels between the *Poetics* and the *Natyashastra* in terms of matter, means, manner and function.

**1. Matter**

If we ask: What is drama? we get an identical answer from both Aristotle and Bharata. To Aristotle drama is "not an imitation of men *per se*, but of human action and of life and happiness and misery" (vi: 48-49). Bharata defines drama as an imitation of people's demeanor, attitudes, conditions, and joys and sorrows:

*Nanabhavosampannam nanavasthantaratkam,*
*Lokavritanukarnam natyametan-mayakritam.*

*Yoyam svabhavo lokasya sukhdukh samanvitah,*
*Soangadyabhinayopeto natyamityabhidhiyate.*

(NS I: 112, 121).

Finally, Bharata defines drama as "an imitation of human action : *Kritanukarnam loke natyamityabhidhiyate*" (NS I: 123).

Two words of this definition of drama require a little consideration. These two words are: *imitation* and *action*. These two words constitute the hinge on which the theory of drama revolves — whether Aristotelian or Bharatiya. What is meant by imitation here? In common parlance, imitation means some sort of copying. An imitation is opposed to the original which it is an imitation of. When someone says that a particular thing or mannerism is an imitation, he is obviously using the word in a pejorative sense. Not only that, such uses necessarily imply that the imitation is dependent upon something else. That is, an imitation borrows its life, its mode of being, from something extraneous and hence it is inferior. This meaning of imitation was originally proposed by Plato in his comments on poetry (cf The *Ion* 534, The *Republic* X). Plato believed that imitation (mimesis) was morally unhygienic and intellectually undependable because it was a copying, a lying, a sort of madness, a distortion of and a removal from reality. Looking back, one really marvels that this meaning of imitation should have survived twenty-four centuries of its continuous and pervasive use, notwithstanding the axiom of linguistic scholarship that language, like its user, is a dynamic organism.

Bharata and Aristotle, however, seem to have used imitation in a technical sense. It is used as the differentia of art in general, and, of drama in particular. It is the imitative element, says a critic, that makes "the poet a poet" (Mckeon 1957). Imitation is used in the *Poetics* and the *Natyashastra* to refer to both the product and the process of the dramatic art. It is not only the finished product, the form, but also the process which produces the form. The process part of imitation is indicated by the term *action*. A drama is not an imitation of a person, thing, or place. It is an imitation of action. Life is a continuity of change and progression. An action is a change, a dynamism, not a statis. Aristotle defines plot as "an imitation of action" (*Poetics* VI: 51). Plot is in drama what action is in life. Plot is an objectification (or concretization) of action. But it is not a mere reproduction or a faithful representation of action. It is a transformation, a recreation. Life is often ugly and painful but art is always pleasurable. If imitation were a faithful representation of the reality of life and its actions, it should have been repulsive. Imitation here refers to the artistic process, to the alchemy that converts the ugly and painful into something which is enjoyable. Aristotle defines plot as "the arrangement of incidents" (VI: 12-18), i.e., as structure, as form, and as such it is called "the first principle" and the *soul* of tragedy (VI: 80-81). It is the structure and the workmanship that makes dramatic representation enjoyable; it is the workmanship that shows the individuality and originality of the artist: "the structure of the plot shows the better poet" (XIV: 2-3). In the earlier chapter Aristotle had made it clear that men find pleasure in imitation, because it is a workmanship. He says:

"There are somethings that distress us when we see them in reality, but the most *accurate* representations of these *same* things we view with pleasure — as for example, the forms of the most despised animals and corpses" (IV: 6-11, italics added).

Again,

"Men will not find any pleasure in the imitation *qua* imitation, but in the *workmanship*" (IV: 18-20).

Bharata's meaning of imitation (*Anukriti*) is evident from the analogies which he uses to describe the process in which aesthetic pleasure is produced. In his prose commentary following verse 32 in chapter VI Bharata says (cf NS VI: 32-36 in Shastri 1972: 282-90).

"Just as various spices and other ingredients produce food with a delicious flavour, similarly, various feelings and emotions combined with dramatic presentation produce a dominant emotion (*Sthayibhava*) which in its fully developed form achieves relishability (*Rasatva*)".

Again,

"Just as the mixing and blending of different ingredients yields a drink with a flavour that is altogether different from that of any of the ingredients, likewise, the proper combination of determinants (*Vibhavas*), consequents (*Anubhavas*) and fleeting emotions (*Vyabhicharibhavas*) produces a dominant emotion (*Sthayibhava*) which provides aesthetic pleasure (*Rasa*)".

Imitation for Bharata means the process and the product of such artistic transcreation. Incidentally, it is refreshing to re-read Eliot's essay on 'Tradition and the Individual Talent' with reference to Bharata's description of the creative process which converts the ordinary human emotion into an aesthetically enjoyable dominant emotion. One is really struck by the variety and extent of the echoes of Bharata's description in this essay. According to Eliot the poet's mind, while engaged in the creative process, "digests and transmutes" passions which are its material. The creative process is a fusion but it is "the intensity of the artistic process, the pressure, so to speak, under which the fusion takes place, that counts". In the creative process varied feelings are not only at liberty to enter into new combinations, but also impressions and experiences combine in "peculiar and unexpected ways" and form a new compound. The poetic process is neither an emotion, nor a recollection, nor a tranquillity of a very great number of experiences and a new thing results from such concentration. Commenting on a certain passage of *The Revenger's Tragedy* (III.IV) of Cyril Tourneur, Eliot refers to the "structural emotion provided by the drama" and observes:

"But the whole effect, the *dominant* tone, is due to the fact that a number of *floating emotions*, having an *affinity* to *this* emotion by no means superficially evident, have combined with it to give us a *new art emotion*" (Eliot, 1953).

Both Bharata and Aristotle recognize the importance of the artistic process which transmutes ordinary experience or emotion into an aesthetic experience or emotion. But the question arises: How is ordinary emotion transformed into an artistic emotion? And it is on this question that Bharata and Aristotle come closer. The process which transforms or depersonalizes ordinary emotion into an artistic emotion is called *Sadharanikarana* (universalization). Both theories believe that an artistic emotion is not local or personal; it is a universalized or depersonalized emotion so that it becomes a pattern or a manifestation of the universal in the specific or of the relation between the universal and the particular.

In academic discussions of poetry it has become fashionable to say with the New Critics that the traditional dichotomy between form and content is unnecessary because art exists only as form and because form embraces and penetrates content (cf Wimsatt and Brooks 1964 : 78). Some critics claim that to "speak of content as such is not to speak of art, at all, but of experience; and that it is only when we speak of the *achieved* content, the form, the work of art as a work of art, that we speak as critics" (Schorer 1972). It is significant to remember in such contexts that the New Critics' doctrine of the inseparability of form and content is only a revival or re-statement of what Aristotle had said about form. In general usage form simply means the shape or structure of something. The form of a poem or of a play, is simply a metaphoric extension of this literal meaning. But in the Aristotelian system form has a much deeper and wider meaning. It is not only shape but that which shapes, not only structure but the principle of structure. In this wide sense form will include both meaning and structure: "Where there is form there will be matter, *informed*; where there is matter there will be form, *informing* ... in the actual thing the two will be a unity, since it is only by their union that the thing exists" (Shipley 1970: 128). In spite of this unity, it is possible to separate the form and the matter for the purposes of academic discussion of art, although we must remember that this separation is only a mental abstraction, not something clearly identifiable in a work of art. In other words, it is possible to use form in these two senses: form as opposed to matter, and form as inclusive of matter. Imitation, as used in the *Poetics* and the *Natyashastra,* refers to both meanings of form, it is both a process and an artefact.

1.1 *Means*

As imitation is the differentia of the fine arts, language is the differentia of the literary art. Since drama is a form of the latter, it is both an imitative and linguistic entity. It has already been pointed out that both Aristotle and Bharata define drama as imitation. When we turn to their formulations about drama as a linguistic entity, we find a certain degree of similarity in the principle of the classification of language varieties used in a dramatic work. In chapter XXI of the *Poetics* words are classified into several categories. Some of these categories are: (i) standard words (ii) ornamental words (iii) ordinary words and (iv) strange words. Likewise, in chapter XVII of the *Natyashastra* (verses 25-29) the author discusses four varieties of language used in drama. Three of these varieties are: (i) the high speech (*Atibhasha*), (ii) the standard speech (*Aryabhasha*) and (iii) the ordinary speech (*Jatibhasha*). Besides, both Aristotle and Bharata discuss the language of drama in terms of (a) speech sounds, (b) words in general and (c) figures of speech (cf Poetics XX-XXII & NS XV-XVII). Both of them define metaphor as a figure of speech which is based on a perception of similarity between two different entities. To quote Aristotle, "the ability to construct metaphor implies the ability to see essential similarity" (XXII: 72-73). According to Bharata, "that whose form is based on similarity is metaphor: *Sadrishya-sampannam yad rupam rupakantu tat*" (XVII: 58). Aristotle's view of metaphor has always been considered a seminal contribution to the development of Poetics. Bharata has traditionally been regarded in India as the earliest and most important authority on metaphor (*rupaka*).

1.2 *Manner*

As imitation is peculiar to the fine arts and language to the art of literature, manner is distinctive of drama when compared to the other forms of literature. Manner is the differentia of drama, since it is through its manner that drama achieves its separate identity as a literary genre. Unlike any other literary genre, drama synthesizes the aural with the visual, the text with presentation. Aristotle's *dramatic manner* and Bharata's *Abhinaya* share a common feature in that they both refer to the process which might be called *dramatization*. It is through the process of dramatization that a play transforms its content into a visual form and creates a dramatic situation. The dramatic manner, as it is used in the *Poetics*, has a much deeper and wider meaning than *spectacle* or the *optical part* (opsis). In the Aristotelian approach the optical part is confined only to *doing* (from the Greek *dran*) or *acting* (from the Greek *prattein*). Opsis is a *part* of tragedy (VI: 35-36) because it requires the means and the agents to *dramatize* the incidents of the plot (III: 34-35). But opsis is not indispensable, for, "the power of tragedy is felt even without a dramatic performance and actors" (VI: 107-108). In other words tragedy can provide "a vivid experience in reading *as well as* in actual performance" (XXVI: 33-37). Dramatic manner, on the other hand, is indispensable to tragedy, to its identity. Tragedy, says Aristotle, *achieves* its effect only through the *dramatic manner* (cf VI: 8-11) and it is because of its dramatic manner that tragedy is superior to epic (XXVI: 37-58). Tragedy achieves its concentration, compactness and unity of artistic effect only through its manner.

Bharata's term for the dramatic manner is *Abhinaya*. Abhinaya is not mere acting. Etymologically, Abhinaya is that which "carries the meaning to the audience" (NS VIII: 6-7). As the technical term in the *Natyashastra*, Abhinaya refers to the whole gamut of features which establishes the uniqueness of drama among the genres of literature. Drama is drama because of Abhinaya: "drama resides in Abhinaya: *Natyasmin pratishthitam*" (NS VIII: 8).

Bharata and Aristotle, alike, extol drama as the best genre of literature. Of the two best developed genres of fourth century Greek literature, Aristotle convincingly asserts the superiority of tragedy to epic in the concluding chapter of the *Poetics* (XXVI: 32-58). According to Bharata, drama occupies the highest position in the hierarchy of literary forms. It is accorded the status of a Veda; it is the fifth Veda, i.e., *Natyaveda* (NS I: 16-19). It is the quintessence of all knowledge, skill, art, spirituality and action; what is not in drama cannot be any one of these:

*Natajnyanam natachhilpam na sa vidya na sa kala,*
*Na sau yogo na tatkarma natyesmin yannadrishyate*
(NS I: 117)

1.3 *Function*

In both the *Natyashastra* and the *Poetics*, the function of drama as the final cause, is related to the achievement of an artistic effect on the audience. Rasa or Catharsis is the technical name given to this function. Rasa and Catharsis have three characteristics in common. These characteristics are: (i) that drama must provide pleasure (ii) that the dramatic variety of pleasure is associated with learning and (iii) that this combination of pleasure and learning emanates from the perception of the relation of the specific to the universal. Since the nucleus of the aesthetic pleasure produced by drama is said to be some sort of illumination in both the systems, Rasa and Catharsis might be seen as somewhat parallel designations of *illuminative pleasure*.

Aristotle identifies the *goal* or the *end* of dramatic imitation with the *emotional* or *artistic effect* that drama seeks to achieve (cf XIII: 24, XIV: 16, XXVI: 38, 55-58) and says that the emotional effect is one of *pleasure*. Aristotle's view that drama should provide *pleasure* (cf XIV: 16) is comparable to Bharata's claim that drama will provide pleasure to the audience: *Vinodkarnam loke natyametadbhavishyati* (NS I: 122).

Aristotle says that drama aims at achieving Catharsis (cf VI: 10), likewise, Bharata holds that drama has no other aim than producing Rasa: *Na hi rasadrite kashchid pyartha pravartate*

(NS VI: 32). Both Aristotle and Bharata offer a psychological explanation for the audience's interest in or enjoyment of dramatic imitation. "All men", says Aristotle, "find pleasure in imitations" (IV: 6). Bharata believes that drama was born out of the natural tendencies of man to imitate and that imitation gives pleasure (cf Rangacharya 1966: 51). According to Bharata, drama is that means of providing pleasure which is worth hearing and witnessing: *Kridaniyakamichchhamo drishyam shravyancha yadbhavet* (NS I: II) because it is an imitation of emotions of all kinds: *trailokyasya sarvasya natyam bhavanukirtanam* (NS I: 107).

What is the nature of the pleasure derivable from drama? Aristotle argues that people find pleasure in viewing dramatic representation because it is an act of *learning* and learning is *pleasant* not only to *philosophers* but to "other men as well". Further, men find pleasure in viewing such representations because it "turns out that they learn and infer what each thing is" (IV: 11-16). Bharata regards drama as the supreme form of knowledge, i.e., *Natyavedam* (NS I: 16). Explaining how drama provides pleasure, Bharata points out that it does so through the imaginative representation of history and through giving knowledge:

*Vedavidyetihasanam akhyanparikalpanam,*
*Vinodkarnam loke natyametadbhavisthyati*

(NS I: 122)

It has already been pointed out that according to the *Natyashastra* the pleasure of a dramatic representation is produced through presenting particular experiences or situations as universalized (*Sadharanikrita*) experiences.

**2. Rasa**

In order to provide an explicit account of Bharata's theory of Rasa, it is necessary to have a clear understanding of some of his basic concepts. Bharata's theory of Rasa is based on a psychological view of the way human personality is constituted. There are certain primary emotions which determine human personality both in its motivation and intellection. These permanent and universal emotions are called *dominant emotions.*

A dramatic composition seeks to build up a particular dominant emotion through a variety of factors. When the dominant emotion created by a dramatic composition is fully developed, it becomes enjoyable because it calls forth the dominant emotion in the mind of the audience. It must, however, be noted, that the dominant emotion attains relishability (*Rasatva*) only when it is aesthetically excited. Rasa is a technical term and it refers to only that kind of enjoyment and pleasure which is brought about through artistic means or situations (cf Dasgupta 1970, Sankaran 1973: 104. Dalal 1973: 109, NS, Vol I, pp 266, 281-82). Bharata himself says that only those dominant emotions which are created and made enjoyable through a dramatic composition qualify for the title of Rasa: *Tasamannatyarasah smritah* (NS I: 34). Strictly speaking, Rasa is the dramatic variety of aesthetic pleasure because Bharata specifically uses the term *Natyarasah.*

Three basic assumptions of Bharata's theory of aesthetic pleasure are: (i) that the only aim of drama is to produce pleasure: *Na bhi rasadrite kashchidpyartha pravartate* (author's commentary following verse 32 in chapter VI of NS), (ii) that such pleasure is based on *Bhava,* i.e., aesthetic emotion, and not vice versa: *Bhavabhyo rasanamabhinir vrittirna tu rasebhyo bhavanamabhinirvrittariti* (prose section following NS VI: 34) and (iii) that it is only a *Sthayibhava* (dominant emotion) that becomes aesthetically enjoyable: *Bhavabhinaya sambandham sthayibhavanstha budhah asvadayanti manasa tasmannatyarasah smritah* (NS VI: 34). Bharata also believes that (aesthetic) emotion and (aesthetic) pleasure are closely interrelated; no aesthetic pleasure can exist without an aesthetic emotion nor can an aesthetic emotion be incapable of aesthetic pleasure: *Na bhavahinosti raso na bhava rasavarjitah* (NS VI: 37). An aesthetic emotion, says Bharata, is that which produces aesthetic pleasure: *Bhavabhavayanti rasan* (NS VI: 36).

Aesthetic emotions are divided into two groups: dominant emotions (*sthayibhavas*) and accessory emotions (*vyabhichari* or *sanchari bhavas*). Accessory emotions are those diverse and fleeting emotions which function to bring about a dominant emotion. The dominant emotion is like that undivided whole of a flame which emerges from those kinetic atoms and flamelets which continually come and go. The accessory emotions are like these continually fleeting flamelets and atoms (cf Dasgupta 1970). But Bharata seems to add by way of an explanation that these fleeting emotions, however important they may be, cannot alone produce a dominant emotion in a dramatic composition. There are two other factors which are needed. These two factors are called *Vibhavas* and *Anubhavas*, often translated as determinants and consequents (cf Keith 1924: 315). A determinant is the objective constituent of an emotion, such as the agents of the dramatic action and the dramatic situations. The agents of the dramatic action constitute *Alambanvibhava* while the dramatic situations constitute what is known as *Uddipanavibhava*. A consequent, on the other hand, is the physical manifestation of a state of mind or of an emotion. A consequent is provided by physical movements and gestures that the agents of the action display. A consequent is therefore related to what Bharata calls *Angic Abhinaya*, i.e., acting or performance. A dramatic composition makes use of three devices to build up a dominant emotion. To put it differently, the development or creation of a dominant emotion is a three-part process. The *Vibhava* is that part which relates to the description of the play as well as to the description of the scenes and circumstances which make certain states of mind capable of being sensed by the audience. The *Anubhava* is concerned with the physical manifestations which make certain states of mind actually sensed by the audience while the Vyabhichirabhivas present the gamut of these diverse, fleeting and accessory emotions which feed and concretize the dominant emotion. Thus it becomes clear that a dominant emotion is produced through the cooperation of determinants, consequents and accessories. Here, we must note, that a dominant emotion is not a simple aesthetic emotion; it is a complex emotion, a pattern or synthesis of diverse elements and that it is brought about through a process of transformation, a transformation in which the constituent elements lose their separate identities and co-operate to take the form of a new whole which is a unity. Such a concept of the aesthetic emotion was perhaps implied by Coleridge when he claimed that imagination had the power of "reducing multitude into a unity of effect, and modifying a series of thoughts by some one predominant thought or feeling" (quoted in Richards 1960: 190-91). When this unified new whole is developed to a climax it becomes maximally pleasurable to the audience. Such a pleasurable experience is Rasa: *Asvadyamantvat* (Prose section immediately preceding verse 33 in NS VI).

Bharata's account of Rasa-realization, however, generated a controversy which continued unabated for centuries. This is because in his famous Rasasutra he does not mention the dominant emotion. Besides, it is an extremely crypic statement. It simply says that aesthetic pleasure is accomplished as a result of the conjunction of determinants, consequents and accessories, *Vibhavanubhava vyabhichari samyogadrasanispattih* (Bharata's formulation following NS VI: 32). This formulation taxed the ingenuity of scholars for a long time as they kept asking questions like: What is the relationship between the Vibhavas, Anubhavas and Vyabhicharibhavas on the one hand and Rasa on the other? Is Rasa a direct result of the combination of the constituent elements? Or does something supervene between the combination of these elements and the coming into being of Rasa? If it is so, why is that intermediate stage not mentioned here? If it is not so, why does Bharata say in chapter VI (verses 33-34 and in the prose section) that it is only a dominant emotion which attains pleasurableness (*Rasatva*)? Respective attempts by scholars to arrive at a convincing explanation of the Rasasutra gave rise to a variety of interpretations. In later times each of these interpretations acquired the status of a theory of Rasa. At least four contending theories of Rasa are generally recognized.

2.1 *Rasa as Production* (Utpatti)

Bhatta Lollata (early ninth century), a follower of the Mimamsa School of philosophy, was the earliest commentator on the *Natyashastra*. He proposed a theory of Rasa which is known as the theory of production (*utpattivada*). According to this view, Rasa is the effect (*utpadya*) of a cause (*karana*). The cause is provided by the combination of the *Vibhavas, Anubhavas* and *Vyabhicharibhavas*. These constituents combine to produce a dominant emotion which is enjoyed by the audience. Bharata's *nispatti* is thus explained as *utpatti*. According to Lollata, the dominant emotion originally belongs to the real hero. Then it passes on to the actor who imitates the real hero in form, dress, and action. Finally, it becomes a source of enjoyment to the spectator who identifies himself with the actor and, through the actor, with the real hero.

Three objections are made against this theory:

(i) Aesthetic pleasure and the witnessing of the play are contemporaneous, but an effect can never be simultaneous with its cause. This means that an effect comes into being only when the cause comes to be, but Rasa cannot be experienced if its constituents are not available.

(ii) Aesthetic experience must be a personal experience of the spectator. Lollata's version of aesthetic pleasure is so diluted that the spectator cannot have a sense of full participation in it.

(iii) The spectator does not know the real hero. The hero he knows is the one who lives in the work of the dramatist. The actor and the so-called real hero become one for the spectator, at least, for the time being. As for the actor having the emotion of the real hero, the spectator simply does not know nor is he interested in it. As far as the spectator is concerned, the actor is merely the means of portraying or exhibiting a certain experience which the dramatist has put into a character.

2.2 *Rasa as Inference* (Anumiti)

In view of the objections to Lollata's theory, an alternative theory of Rasa was expounded by a Naiyayika, named Shri Shankuka, about the middle of the ninth century. This theory interprets Bharata's *nispatti* as *anumiti* and is therefore called the theory of inference (*Anumiti-vada*). Shankuka contends that Rasa is not *Produced;* rather it is *inferred*. The dominant emotion is inferred to exist in the mind of the actor by means of the *Vibhavas, Anubhavas* and *Vyabhicharibhavas*. Since the spectator identifies himself with the actor, the emotion thus inferred in the mind of the latter, develops into something relishable. The realization of Rasa, Shankuka argues, is simply an experience of logical inference, though an inference very different from ordinary inference. The experience of aesthetic pleasure, though inferential, is not fully unreal. This experience is partly real and unreal. It is a form of knowledge which is based on what Shankuka calls *chitra-turag-nyaya,* i.e., a metaphoric way of calling a horse in a painting a horse. This form of knowledge provides pleasure through its being connected with *Vibhavas, Anubhavas* and *Vyabhicharibhavas*. This unique form of inferential knowledge accounts for the spectator's cognitional ambivalence towards the object of his aesthetic pleasure. The spectator knows that what he sees is not real, yet believes that it is. Shankuka holds that the truth of art cannot be rejected as philosophically unsound or intellectually uncertain. This is a sort of truth or reality where the spectator experiences what Coleridge calls "the willing suspension of disbelief".

Shankuka's theory, however, has its own share of limitations. It does not, for example, show how the spectator can know whether the actor has real feelings or whether he is merely feigning. Secondly, like its predecessor, this theory also presupposes that the dominant emotion is transferred to the spectator (inferentially though). But the third and the most crucial objection to this theory is concerned with its basic hypothesis itself. Can inference produce real aesthetic pleasure? It is a matter of common experience that the realization of thrill or joy is personal and immediate. It is a matter of direct perception or participation. It cannot be achieved through any inferential or derivative mode of knowledge.

2.3 *Rasa as Enjoyment* (Bhoga)

More than a century after Shankuka, yet another view of Rasa called the theory of Aesthetic Enjoyment (*Bhuktivada*), was put forward by Bhatta Nayaka, an adherent of the Samkhya School of philosophy. This theory forcefully denies that Rasa is a production or an inference or a revelation. The most powerful and notable contribution of Nayaka's theory is his conceptualization of a highly useful theoretical construct to explain the peculiar nature of aesthetic experience. How is it that aesthetic experience is always pleasurable? How does a dramatic representation of even a painful and ugly experience give joy to the audience?

Nayaka's theory postulates a three-fold function of poetic language: (i) the significative function (*Abhidha*) which deals with what is expressed, (ii) the unificatory function (*Bhavakatva*) which relates to aesthetic pleasure and (iii) the realisationistic function (Bhojakatva or Bhoga) which has regard to the audience (cf Sankaran 1973: 103, De 1959: 200 & Keith 1924: 317). It should be noted that Nayaka's *Abhidha* is not mere denotation or reference; it includes *Lakshana,* i.e., connotation or emotiveness as well. According to Nayaka, most uses of language perform the significative function. Poetry (or drama) distinguishes itself from ordinary language in respect of the second and the third functions. Explaining the second function of poetic language, Nayaka attempts to answer questions like those posed above. His formulation of the concept of *Sadharanikarana* (universalization) takes care of the difficulties which a theory of Rasa must overcome and which relates to the individualistic element of the spectator's experience and to the enjoyment of the otherwise painful experiences. A poetic description or a dramatic representation, Nayaka argues, offers the dominant emotion and its constituents in their universalized characters and without any reference to their local or specific properties. An aesthetic emotion is intrinsically different from a personal, real and ordinary emotion. When the spectator (*Sahirdaya*), i.e., one of kindred heart), through his imaginative sympathy, identifies himself with what he witnesses (or reads) and thereby loses his personal predilections. The spectator is absolutely attuned to what he sees and hears and is, for the time being, freed from "time, place and causality" (cf Gnoli 1970) and hence is liberated from the string of painful emotions. What he witnesses is not local or particular, therefore, not chaotic; but is universal and eternal and, therefore, harmonious. When the dramatic experience is thus universalized, the third function of poetic language starts operating. It is the third function that enables the spectator to call forth the corresponding innate emotion or experience in him and to develop it in consonance with the dramatic emotion to a climax where it becomes Rasa in the form of self-illumination.

It is important to bear in mind that Nayaka was a believer in Samkhya philosophy and as such it is very likely that he related the third function of poetic language to the Samkhya concept of *Sattva Guna,* i.e., the luminous component of human personality. *Sattva* is that element or component of our personality which enables us to go upwards because it is of the nature of pleasure, buoyancy and luminosity (cf Chatterjee and Dutta 1960: 261). It is, Nayaka would argue, because of these two processes of universalization and realization that aesthetic experience is always joyous. The employment of aesthetic emotion is a process of delectation. Great poetry or great drama transports us to a higher plane of living by energizing the Sattva inherent in us. Nayaka's third function of poetic language reminds one of Longinus's view that sublimity consists in the ability of great poetry to create in the reader a sense of being instantaneously carried away to new heights of passionate experience. Not only that, Nayaka's *Sahirdaya* seems to be the first cousin of Longinus' experienced and sympathetic reader.

The main objection to Nayaka's theory is that it attributes to poetic language two additional functions: viz *Bhavakatva* and *Bhojakatva*, without any legitimate basis. As a matter of fact, they are not functions of poetic language; they are related to the poetic process and to the psychology of the audience, respectively. As *Bhavakatva* and *Bhojakatva* do not relate to the function of poetic language, they should not have been treated at par with *Abhidha* and *Lakshana*.

2.4 *Rasa as Manifestation* (Abhivyakti)

The fourth and final view of Rasa was propounded by the Vedantist scholar, Abhinavaguptacharya (Abhinava for short), towards the end of the tenth century or the beginning of the eleventh century. This view is discussed in all its details in the *Abhinavabharati* and is known as the theory of Manifestation (*Abhivyaktivada*). The *Abhinavabharati* is not only the most learned and comprehensive commentary on the *Natyashastra*; it is the only source of information about what earlier commentators like Lollata, Shankuka and Nayaka wrote on Bharata's Rasasutra. All later writings on Rasa have attempted to interpret and elaborate what Abhinava wrote on the Rasasutra in the sixth chapter of his commentary (quoted in full Shastri 1972: 229-284 and in De 1959: 219-235). Abhinava's theory of Rasa has not yet been superseded by any other view. Abhinava accepts Nayaka's concept of universalization and his view that Rasa relates to the experience of the spectator. But he rejects Nayaka's claim that poetic language distinguishes itself from ordinary language by virtue of the twin functions of *Bhavakatva* and *Bhojakatva*. According to Abhinava, the uniqueness of poetic language resides in suggestion (*Vyanjana*). Poetry both expresses and suggests but it is the latter which distinguishes it from all other uses of language. The poet is both a "seer" (*Rishi*) and a "maker" (*Kavi* cf Raghavan 1965). The poet is at once he who sees and he who is able to express what he sees (cf Gnoli 1970). But the real success of the poet lies in *suggesting* what he *does not* express, though what he suggests is gathered from what he expresses. This process of suggestion is the essence of poetry and it is in this that the experienced and responsive reader (the *Sahirdaya*) discovers the secret of his joy of aesthetic experience.

Abhinava assigns universalization to the process of the artistic transformation of an ordinary, real-life emotion, into an aesthetic emotion. The artistic process converts a personal emotion into a *universalized* or generic emotion, a painful emotion into a pleasurable emotion. The aesthetic emotion is pleasurable because it is a universalized emotion. It is, at once, the emotion of a moment and of all time, of a person and of all people, of a place and of all places. It is an emotion in which one becomes all and all become one. It is local yet universal, temporal yet timeless, painful yet enjoyable.

In the exposition of his theory of Rasa Abhinava elaborates Nayaka's view that Rasa is a personal experience for the spectator. But he does not follow Nayaka's way. According to Abhinava, Rasa relates to the psychology of the audience. It is he who propounds the view that the human personality is constituted both in its motivation and intellection by certain primary emotions which are innate in man and which lie dormant in the subconscious or unconscious strata of his psyche. As these primary emotions are universally and permanently stored in all human beings, they may be called dominant emotions or *sthayibhavas*. However, these emotions are not relishable unless they are evoked through dramatic representations (or through other artistic means). When a play presents a dominant emotion in its most developed form through the synthesis of *Vibhavas*, *Anubhavas* and *Vyabhicharibhavas*, the spectator has an experience of joy as the dramatic emotion calls forth or manifests his own dominant emotion. The spectator's aesthetic pleasure is based on the manifestation (*Abhivyakti*) of that joy which is in the true nature of the self. Rasa is the manifestation of the essential identity between the spectator's own individual emotion and the emotion of art. The spectator's experience of such pleasure is "nothing else but the enlightenment of a universal" (Dasgupta 1970).

One of the characteristic merits of the theory of manifestation is that it distinguishes aesthetic pleasure both from ordinary pleasure as well as from spiritual ecstasy. The essence of Rasa, according to Abhinava, is that it is a pleasure which has no relationship with any particular ego. It is free from all local or individual interferences. It is a pleasure which emanates from a universalized, generic and disinterested emotion. At the same time, aesthetic pleasure is clearly different from spiritual ecstasy. Spiritual bliss is absolute and transcendent but aesthetic pleasure has a material basis. As it cannot come into being without *Vibhavas*, *Anubhavas* and *Vyabhicharibhavas* brought together in a dramatic representation (or any artistic representation), it cannot be absolute. Rasa is relative in yet another sense. It depends for its existence on an artistic basis and is contemporaneous with it. As Rasa is realized only through being simultaneous with a dramatic or artistic representation, it cannot be perennial (cf Gnoli 1970 & Nagendra 1970). Aesthetic joy is comparable to spiritual joy. It is, to quote Tagore, a "foretaste of spiritual realization" (Raghavan 1965); but it is not the same as spiritual joy.

### 3. **Catharsis** (Katharsis)

In his short preface to the Oxford Edition of the *Rhetoric* (*The Works of Aristotle*, Vol XI) W R Roberts (1946: V) suggests: "In the last two words of the *Poetics*, as it has come down to us, we may fancy that we hear Aristotle quietly taking leave of all the science, logic, the metaphysics, and the political and moral wisdom that have gone before . . . . . let it suffice to have said *thus much*" (italics added).

If we agree with Roberts that the *Poetics* was the last work of Aristotle, then what Aristotle says in this book acquires a special significance, particularly in regard to the present topic of discussion, more so when we know that Aristotle was a systematic thinker. Anyone who is familiar with Aristotle's writings will agree that the Aristotelian approach to any subject that he deals with is characterized by what Davies (1965: 32) calls "a logical symmetry", i.e., a system which has an inter-connection among its constituent statements. Aristotle's propositions about a particular science constitute a scientific system because they are related to one another through their internal consistency and through being concerned with the same subject. When we discuss Aristotle's theory of drama which forms part of his theory of imitative arts in general, we must remember that, in keeping with the Aristotelian system, it is a set of premises, a postulational system, from which empirical laws are deducible as theorems. One of the characteristics of the system, Mckeon (1957) tells us, is that it employs a special terminology and has its terms rigorously defined so that the statements which constitute the theory are precise and not vague. Mckeon also suggests that the meaning of a technical term must be determined in relation to the other terms within the same *science* because the same term may mean different things in different *sciences* that Aristotle divided his works into. This means that the meaning of a technical term in the *poetic* sciences has to be determined with reference to the other terms which occur only in the *Poetics* and the *Rhetoric*, as they are the only works which belong to the *science of making* (Poetike). It also needs to be noted that in the *Poetics*, as in most other writings, Aristotle follows the deductive method of moving from *making* (most general) to *imitation* (less general) to *literature* (specific) and finally to *tragedy* (most specific, cf Golden & Hardison 1968: 65).

The catharsis clause of Aristotle's famous definition of tragedy has been one of the most (perhaps the most) vigorously debated clauses in the history of Western poetics. Two factors seem to have created the main butt of the controversies: first, the polysemism of the term Catharsis, and secondly, Aristotle's mystifying silence on what he exactly meant by this term in the *Poetics*. His silence became more inscrutable in view of what he had written in the *Politics*: "the sense of the term (Katharsis) will be explained in our lectures on poetics, but may be left to speak for itself at the moment" (1341[b]). That catharsis was left to *speak for itself* even in the *Poetics* naturally generated unending controversies, and even today, one cannot be sure of its *exact* meaning. But before we proceed with a review of the various views of Catharsis, it is necessary to cite the clause that contains the term: "with incidents arousing pity and fear, wherewith to accomplish its catharsis of such emotions" (VI 9-10 Bywater's translation of the *Poetics* (1449) in *Works* vol XI). A careful reading of the *Poetics* will reveal that a sense of duality pervades the work at every stage of its argument. Some of the dualities are: pity and fear, happiness and misery, good fortune and bad fortune, ignorance and knowledge, simple plots and complex plots, happy and unhappy endings, *Oedipus* and *Iphigenia,* the two occurrences of Catharsis, and, finally, conflict and reconciliation. To have a clear perspective of Aristotelian thought, it is important to read with the Catharsis clause the shorter definition of tragedy where the author says that it is an imitation of "human action and life and *happiness* and misery"(VI: 49 italics added). Similarly, in chapter XI Aristotle mentions both *Oedipus* and *Iphigenia* to illustrate his notion of a complex plot in which recognition occurs with reversal and observes that such "a recognition and reversal will evoke pity and fear, . . . . and furthermore, happiness and misery will appear in circumstances of this type" (21-24). Again in chapter XVII (40-43) where catharsis is used for the second and last time, it is associated with Orestes' *deliverance* as his *madness* is linked with his *capture*. If we have all these remarks in mind, can we say that they have a logical symmetry? Reading drama from the point of view of means and ends, can we say that the Aristotelian conception of tragedy includes both conflict and reconciliation, and relates pity and fear or happiness and misery, or madness, to the conflict part, i.e., the means, and catharsis to the reconciliation part, i.e., the end result?, Is it logically valid to say that Aristotelian tragedy deals with conflict, heterogeneity, multeity, chaos or contradiction as its themes or as its theme, and seeks to achieve a single, unified and unifying vision as its end? What does Aristotle mean by catharsis? What is the relationship between pity and fear, or happiness and misery, or madness on the one hand, and catharsis on the other? By associating catharsis to such terms, does the author point to the paradoxical nature of aesthetic pleasure? By using catharsis only twice in the *Poetics* (cf chapter VI: 10-11 & chapter XVII: 43) does Aristotle suggest two types of aesthetic pleasure, corresponding to the effects evoked by *Oedipus* and *Iphigenia* respectively? Is catharsis a feature of the structure of tragedy (cf XIV: 15-16) or is it related to the *emotional effect* (cf XIII: 24) of the fictionalized *situation* of tragedy on the audience? Or is it related to both, that is, to the dramatic situation as well as to the psychology of the audience? Is catharsis essentially an experience of pleasure? Is it an act of learning or illumination? Or, is it pleasurable because it is illuminative? What does the illumination consist in? Does it consist in some kind of information or in the enlightenment of a universal or of a hidden pattern?

It is time to take a quick survey of the various interpretations of catharsis with reference to the questions posed above. Available views of catharsis can easily be divided into the following groups.

### 3.1 *Catharsis as Purgation*

The interpretation of catharsis as purgation is basically a medical or homeopathic view. Purgation in such an interpretation means exclusion, elimination, removal, eradication, casting off, or getting rid of something that is certainly harmful. Tragedy, on this view, is considered useful as it helps us purge the harmful emotions of pity and fear, thereby restoring "calm of mind, all passion spent" (*Samson Agonistes*: 67). Proponents of the hygienic or homeopathic or purgation theory of catharsis believe that "like drives out like", for example, one applies heat to cure a fever and cold to cure chills. These proponents also believe that Aristotle borrowed this term from the

Hippocratic medical literature of Greece and employed it as a medical methaphor to explain the function of tragedy (cf Ency Brit Micro, Vol 2, 639). Tragedy, they urge, brings about a purgation, i.e., exclusion of the unhealthy emotions of pity and fear by aggravating them. This interpretation of catharsis is identical with the age-old, popular belief in India that "poison cures poison: *Vishashya vishamaushadham*".

In ancient Greece catharsis was used as a technical term in the writings of the Hippocratic school of Medicine (cf Wheelwright 1965). Members of this school believed that sickness was caused by an excess of certain bodily elements and that health depended on the right proportion among the necessary elements of the body. Under this method of treatment, a sick man had to undergo two processes to regain his health. These two processes were known as *digestion* (pepsis) and *discharge* (katharsis). Digestion was produced by the body's heat, wherein the elements of the body were recombined and fused in such a way that waste products were generated and became ready for discharge. When this discharge took place, the result was right proportion of bodily elements and that was health.

Those who subscribe to the homeopathic view of catharsis believe that tragedy arouses pity and fear only to drive them out. This view draws inspiration from a passage in the *Politics* where catharsis is used in the sense of purgation. Discussing the place of music in the ideal State, Aristotle argues that those who are "influenced by pity and fear" must listen to music to have these emotions "purged (or catharated) and their souls lightened and delighted" (1314[b]). In the preceding chapter of the same book Aristotle says that the flute should be used only on "those occasions when the effect to be produced is the release of emotions" (Katharsis, 1341[a]).

One of the immediate attractions of the hygienic theory is that it makes Aristotle's theory of catharsis a direct retort to Plato's castigation of poets and their profession. In the well-known passage in the tenth book of the *Republic* Plato observes:

"Poetry feeds and waters the passions instead of drying them up, she lets them rule, although they ought to be controlled, if mankind are ever to increase in happiness and virtue" (quoted in Daiches 1956: 19).

Considered in the light of Plato's remark, the catharsis clause in the *Poetics* can be seen as an emphatic asservation that the so-called anarchy and tumult in the psyche caused by poetry's "feeding and watering of the passions" cannot be assuaged or prevented by starving and repressing them. The only way to restore the rule of law in the strife-torn and mutiny-prone psyche of the would-be ideal citizen of the ideal republic is to so much rouse the passions, i.e., emotions, that they are worked off. The easiest and the most efficacious way of bringing about such a much desired return to normalcy in the kingdom of the human psyche is afforded by tragedy.

The purgation theory of catharsis found its most eloquent and influential advocate in John Milton who offered a very lucid and succint account of what Aristotle meant by catharsis. In the opening lines of his Preface to *Samson Agonistes* (1671) Milton says:

"Tragedy ... hath been ... said by Aristotle to be of power by raising pity and fear, or terror, to purge the mind of those and such like passions, that is, to temper and reduce them to just measure with a kind of delight, stirred up by reading or seeing those passions well initiated. Nor is nature wanting in her own effects to make good his assertion, for so in physic things of melancholic hue and quality are used against melancholy, sour against sour, salt to remove salt humours" (ed Davis 1968: 3).

Breuer and Freud added a fresh currency to the purgation theory of catharsis by introducing it into their *Studies on Hysteria* (1895) to describe a method of treatment by which the patient was made to remember, under hypnosis, the circumstances under which her symptoms originated. The patient was also urged to express her emotions accompanying the circumstances and was thereby relieved of hysteric symptoms. This technique of psychotherapy was called the "talking cure" or the "cathartic method" (cf Robert 1966: 82-85 and Jones 1961: 202-3). Freud gradually gave up hypnotism and developed instead a technique of concentration which he called "psychic analysis" (cf Robert 1966: 84) under which the patient was asked to lie down with closed eyes and to concentrate on a particular symptom and to try to recall everything which, Freud hoped, might explain the origin of the symptom. Freud believed that by recalling the origin of the symptom the patient was catharated or cured of it because Freud was sure that psychoneurosis could be cured only by enabling the patient to give a free expression to the emotions associated with a particular symptom. Pepper (1980) gives the following account of the Freudian interpretation of Catharsis:

".... in dealing with extreme mental conflicts and emotional sufferings, man is endowed with a protective capacity to inhibit them so that they do not have to rise into full consciousness. They, nevertheless, are really not forgotten but, lying in the back of the mind as complexes, constantly seek relief, often coming up in weird disguises in dreams. There is a satisfaction in such relief, and one of the ways of getting it — without having to face the full consciousness of a trauma held back by the inhibitions — is through what are called tragic works of art. In a round-about-way men enjoy the horrors depicted because, without being fully aware of why, they thereby obtain relief from similar experiences they have had themselves and have inhibited but that constantly tend to express themselves. Tragic art is thus, as Aristotle put it, like a purge for pent-up emotions".

It will be obvious from the forgoing resume' of the homeopathic theory of catharsis that undesirable emotions must not be allowed to fester inside man and that they must be driven out. Tragedy, the adherents of this theory argue, has a peculiar power to offer relief to the spectator (or the reader) as it "siphons off these disturbing inner states rather than letting them grow rancid within man" (Hospers 1980). A close scrutiny of this theory, however, raises certain problems:

(a) It attempts to determine the meaning of catharsis by referring it to the sciences extraneous to the poetic sciences. Sources like the writings of the Hippocratic School of Medicine, Plato's *Republic* and Aristotle's *Politics* cannot ensure a correct interpretation of the term. It is perfectly possible for a particular term to occur in two systems of thought or in two disciplines and yet to have two entirely different meanings.

(b) To interpret catharsis as a medical metaphor is to presume a necessary relationship between emotions like pity and fear on the one hand, and tragedy on the other. What kind of relationship does hold between emotions like these and a fortunate tragedy like *Iphigenia in Tauris*? How do they relate to the experience of "happiness and misery"?

(c) Does this theory fully explain the psychology of the audience? Do we equate relief with pleasure? Does the spectator feel *empty* or *full* after witnessing a tragedy?

(d) Is catharsis in itself pleasure or does it lead to pleasure?

(e) Isn't it possible to achieve catharsis through means other than tragedy, say, by taking some drugs or through yogic exercises? If so, how does tragedy distinguish itself as a relief — inducing mechanism from such other mechanisms?

(f) Assuming that tragedy has a curative effect on neurotics, is it not legitimate to ask: what kind of effect does tragedy have on *emotionally healthy* and well organised people? Besides, is everyone, who enjoys a tragedy, a *sick* man, a man who is desperately looking for a treatment to siphon off his psychoneurosis? Or, is it that tragedy helps only those who have a chaotic or punctured psyche, and, that it gives nothing to those who are neurologically enviable? But why do psychologically balanced people enjoy witnessing tragedy?

(g) The world of man, like the world of tragedy, comprises a heterogeneous population, but the purgation theory of catharsis presupposes a unitary world (in both senses) in which *all* tragedies have the *same* effect on *all* people.

(h) Finally, does tragedy provide *relief* or does it provide *ecstasy* to the spectator (or reader)?

### 3.2 *Catharsis as Purification or Lustration*

Many scholars believe that there is nothing intrinsically undesirable or harmful about the emotions of pity and fear. These emotions pose a kind of threat to the religious or moral health of people only when they get polluted. It therefore becomes imperative to purify these contaminated and contaminating emotions but not to drive them out; once purified, they deserve to be retained. This sort of purification can best be brought about by tragedy and this view leads to the formulation of what is called the purification or lustration theory of catharsis.

Advocates of the purification theory of catharsis trace the earliest source and sanction of their interpretation in the dialogues of Plato — as for example, in the *Phaedo* and in the *Sophist*. In the *Phaedo* Socrates tells Simmias:

"And purification (catharsis) ..... consists in separating the soul as much as possible from the body, and accustoming it to withdraw from all contact with the body and concentrate itself by itself, and to have it dwelling, alone by itself from the shackles of the body" ($67^d$). Similarly, the Stranger tells Theaetetus in the *Sophist* that there are two sorts of purification, viz, the purification of the body and the purification of the soul and that he prefers that kind of "purification which is concerned with the soul" ($227^c$-$231^b$).

On the basis of such remarks of Plato, some scholars (cf Wheelwright 1965) suggest that Aristotle took the moral/religious meaning of catharsis from his teacher and applied it to the function of tragedy. Catharsis according to this interpretation, is equated with what Aristotle calls *moral virtue*. In the *Nicomachean Ethics*, for example, he argues that moral health is a mean between two extremes:

"..... virtue must have the quality of the intermediate. I mean moral virtue, for it is this that is concerned with passions and actions, and in these there is excess, defect and the intermediate. For instance, both fear and confidence, and appetite and anger and pity and, in general pleasure and plain may be felt too much and too little, and in both cases not too well; but to feel them at the right times with reference to the right objects forward to the right people, with the right motive, and in the right way, is what is characteristic and best, and this is the characteristic of virtue" (1106[b]).

Incidentally, making allowances for the difference between the moral and the spiritual realms of human experience, it might be tempting to compare Aristotle's doctrine of the *intermediate* with the Buddhistic doctrine of *moderation* or the *middle path*. According to the doctrine of the *middle path*, a man should not follow extremes; namely, self-indulgence and self-mortification. Avoiding these two extremes, Lord Buddha discovered the *middle path* (Majjima patipada) leading to vision, to knowledge, to calmness, to awakening, to Nirvana. This middle path is known as the Noble Eightfold Path consisting of "right view, right thought, right speech, right action, right mode of living, right endeavour, right mindfulness and right concentration" (Rahula 1980).

A fascinating aspect of the lustratory view of catharsis, like that of the purgation view, is that it is a direct rebuttal of Plato's denunciation of the so-called demoralizing effects of poetry. Advocates of this theory regard catharsis as the moral metaphor and assert the view that poetry (including tragedy, of course) has a civilizing, ennobling and edifying effect on its readers.

There emerged, in course of time, a number of variations on the purification theory of catharsis. In the Italian Renaissance, writers like Robertelli (1548) and Castelvetro (1570) advanced "the hardening theory", by which tragedy was said to accustom "the spectator to scenes of misery and violence, hence to harden his weak inclinations to fear and to pity" (Shipley 1970: 30). Castelvetro compared the experience of spectators at witnessing tragedy to the experience of soldiers on the battlefield. Just as the soldiers overcome their fear of death after seeing it frequently on the battlefield, so spectators become *hardened* to the pitiable and fearful events of life by witnessing them in tragedy.

In Germany, Lessing (1768) emphasized the applicability of Aristotle's ethical standard of *due measure* to the principle of catharsis, for tragedy, if it is to transform our pity and fear into virtue, must be capable of *purifying* us from both extremes—from "too little by its emotional contagion", and from "too much by the restraint which its formal pattern imposes" (Wheelwright 1965). Lessing's explanation of catharsis is echoed in the twentieth century by Elizabeth Schneider (1939) who argues that just because pity and terror are painfully and utterly irreconcilable in real life, the one always driving the other out, we receive the greatest pleasure from their *stylized union* in art (Wheelwright 1965). According to Schneider the emotions of pity and fear are rendered reconcilable to each other only because they are transformed or stylized by art. This view need not be confused with the view of synthesis which will follow this section. Stylization in Schneider's interpretation is equivalent to moderation in Lessing's. Both stylization and moderation imply purification.

Yet another version of the lustratory view of catharsis was suggested by Milton in *the Reason of Church Government* (1642). Justifying the reason for the being of poetry, Milton claims that it has "the power to inbreed and cherish in a great people the seeds of virtue and publick civility, to allay the perturbations of the mind, and set the affections in *right tune*" (*ed* Patrides 1974: 57, italics added).

It should be evident from the foregoing review that the purification theory of catharsis is more fascinating than the purgation theory for two reasons. First, it does not entail any elimination of the emotions of pity and fear, rather, it assures that these emotions are purified only to be retained. The spectator's cathartic experience is a hot bath rather than an evacuation. Secondly, the purification theory claims that poetry does not only teach, it also pleases and, it pleases as it teaches. The view that poetry combines pleasure with teaching has had a long history from Horace to Johnson because it turned out to be a natural corollary of the interpretation of catharsis in terms of purification. Aristotle was regarded as the progenitor of the moral notions about poetry. Ever since Horace announced his finely ambiguous formula that the end of poetry was "to instruct or to delight or both" (Rogarson 1972), critics have sought to explain the dual function of poetry in terms of pleasure and profit, and in so doing, they have not only disposed of Plato's moral reservations about poetry, but have also made an additional claim that, over and above, its moral qualities, poetry has a pleasure-giving device. A look at the following remarks will illustrate this point:

(i) "Delightful teaching is the end of poesie"

— Sir Philip Sidney

(ii) "Poetry instructs as it delights"

— John Dryden

(iii) "The end of poetry is to instruct by pleasing"

— Samuel Johnson (quoted in Sharma 1979: 43)

In course of time, certain interpretations of catharsis took the form of a dogmatic assertion. Thomas Taylor, for example, was sure that by 'catharsis' Aristotle meant purification and nothing else. As Taylor says in his edition (1818) of the *Poetics*:

"Aristotle meant to say, that the terror and pity excited by tragedy purify the spectator from those perturbations which form the catastrophe of the tragedy".

(cited in Golden & Hardison 1968: 137)

According to the adherents of the lustratory interpretation of catharsis the joy of reading or witnessing tragedy is based on its purifying capacity. In our own century, critics like Butcher (1907), Hospers (1980) and Wheelwright (1965) support this interpretation of catharsis. Tragedy is great because it offers a vision *distilled* from suffering: man is *pathei mathos* — taught by suffering, as the Chorus in the *Agamemnon* sings (cited in Wheelwright 1965). To sum up the review of this view of catharsis, it should be pointed out that the purification theory, like the purgation theory, raises more problems than it solves:

(a) Like the purgation theory, this theory is also based on the interpretation of catharsis with reference to its meaning in other disciplines.

(b) It also makes Aristotle's theory a derivative of Plato's theory of poetry. Such interpretations deny the kind of independence that Aristotle's theory deserves.

(c) A careful reading of the *Poetics* does not in any way support a didactic doctrine of tragedy. Any attempt to moralize Aristotle's catharsis, as it occurs in the *Poetics*, should be considered a distortion, both unwarranted and indefensible.

(d) What does tragedy do to those who already have stabilized at the intermediate?

(e) This theory does not seem to be in keeping with Aristotle's intellectual explanation of the function of tragedy, for, like the other one, it is an explanation of catharsis in emotive terms.

### 3.3 *Catharsis as Synthesis*

I A Richards made an extraordinarily bold claim when he asserted in 1924 that the two pillars upon which a "theory of criticism must rest are an account of value and an account of communication" (1960: 17). Within the Ricardian framework *value* refers to the structure of aesthetic experience. The most valuable experience is that which *involves* "the widest and most comprehensive co-ordination of impulses and the least curtailment, conflict, starvation and suppression" (p 45). Richards believes that a growing order is the principle of the mind and that the conduct of life is throughout "an attempt to organize impulses" (p 35). An aesthetic experience is valuable not because it is a thing *sui generis*, i.e., something different in *kind* from ordinary human experience but because it achieves a better organization or a greater systematization of impulses and thereby leads the human mind from a chaotic to an organized state. According to Richards, criticism is concerned with the structure of the response that a work of art calls forth in the mind of the reader, not with the structure of the stimulating object, i.e., a work of art. Discussing the effect of art, Richards categorically points out: "the balance is not in the structure of the stimulating object, but it is in the response" (p 196).

What does art do? Richards' answer is very simple: it brings about a systematization of impulses in the mind of the reader or spectator. Terms like balance, poise, organization, systematization, equilibrium, synaesthesis and synthesis, are used almost synonymously to describe the structure of aesthetic experience. In his discussion of 'imagination' in the *Principles of Literary Criticism* (chapter 32) he equates his theory of synthesis with Coleridge's theory of the Imagination and with Aristotle's theory of catharsis. Coleridge, as we all know, defines imagination as a synthetic and magical power which reveals itself in "the balance or reconciliation of opposite or discordant qualities" (quoted in Richards 1960: 190). Tragedy, according to Richards, is the best instance of such balance or reconciliation of "pity, the impulse to approach and terror, the impulse to retreat". "Their union" says Richards, "in an ordered single response is the catharsis by which tragedy is recognized" (ibid 193). Tragedy is the best means of bringing about a synthesis of impulses, for, the tragic experience is "the most general, all-accepting, all-ordering experience" (pp 193-194).

It is, however, interesting to note that in his explanation of synthesis, imagination and catharsis, Richards makes two striking points. These are that (i) the resolution of multeity into unity relates to the "single ordered response" of the reader (or spectator), not to the structure of tragedy (cf pp 192-195) and that (ii) the balance or poise that characterizes such "ordered response" is not peculiar to tragedy: it is a general characteristic of all the most valuable experiences of the arts. It can be given by "a Carpet or a Pot or by a gesture as unmistakably as by the Parthenon, it may come about through an epigram as clearly as through a Sonata" (p 195).

If we carefully examine Richards' theory of Catharsis, we

arrive at the following conclusions: (i) Catharsis is a purely subjective experience of the reader because it is only he who knows what his *ordered* experience is like. Assuming that it is so, the theory becomes vulnerable because it does not explain how that ordered experience is brought about. How does the reader's response relate to the structure of the art object? What features of the *stimulating object* cause that experience? This view of catharsis runs counter not only to that view which considers catharsis an objective entity, but to Richards' earlier position as well. In an earlier chapter of the same book he had said that the work of art is the best evidence of recorded values and that the arts "supply the best data available for deciding what experience are more valuable than others" (p 23). If a work of art is valuable, it must contain within itself the reasons which make it valuable and if it causes certain experiences in the reader, the features of the reader's experience must be explicity relatable to certain features of the work of art. As Richards himself puts it: a full critical statement is that which explains "not only that an experience is valuable in certain ways, but also that it is caused by certain features in a contemplated object" (p 15). (ii) One may surmise that Aristotle uses catharsis, in all probability, to designate the functional differentia of art in general and of tragedy in particular. But the onus lies on the interpreter to explain how tragedy distinguishes itself from other art forms in creating the effect that it does. Richard's view does not do this. By simply equating tragic catharsis with other forms of catharsis, this view makes it a vacuous concept.

(iii) Above all, by confining catharsis to what happens in the nervous system, Richards makes it a neurological metaphor rather than a theory of literature or drama. As he says: "The joy which is so strangely the heart of the tragic experience is not an indication that all's right with the world' or that' somewhere, somehow, there is justice, it is an indication that all is right here and now in the nervous system" (Richards 1960: 193).

3.4 *Catharsis as Illumination*

Leon Golden proposed a radical interpretation of catharsis in his article ("Catharsis") published in 1962 in *Transactions of the American Philological Association* (TAPA, No XcIII, pp 51-60). A few years later, Golden also prepared a translation of the *Poetics* for which O B Hardison (Jr) wrote an excellent commentary incorporating Golden's interpretation of Catharsis. The translation and the commentary were then "collated and both were modified" and published in one volume in 1968. In their joint Preface to this edition of the *Poetics,* the authors claim "objectivity, clarity and suggestivity" (p V). They further add that the two guiding principles of the translation are "accuracy and readability" and that the general aim of the commentary is a consistent readable analysis, original in outline but eclectic and representative in treatment of specific topics" (p VI). For them catharsis means a `clarification of the incidents' of tragedy, "an enhanced understanding of the events depicted in tragedy" (p 116). The tragic poet achieves the clarification of the incidents by "universalizing" the particular and the individual. Universalization is the process which transforms the chaotic, unconnected and unintelligible "singulars" into an intelligible set of universals by discovering or revealing the pattern or interconnection underlying the unrelated, heterogeneous particulars (cf 289-90).This interpretation of catharsis is called the "clarification theory" of catharsis (cf p 117). It might also be called the Golden-Hardison theory of Catharsis, because it is proposed by Golden and supported by Hardison, as also because the two have collated their views in the volume under reference.

The Golden-Hardison view of catharsis has three important characteristics. First, it clearly denies that Aristotle's doctrine of catharsis has anything "didactic" in it (cf 119). Secondly, it makes the catharsis clause a reference to "the techne of tragedy, not to the psychology of the audience", besides relating it to the general theory of imitation outlined in chapters I-IV and to the discussion of probability and necessity in chapter IX (cf 117). Thirdly, it treats of catharsis in purely "intellectual terms — in terms of learning" and advocates that to Aristotle art is learning and learning is pleasure (p 117).

Among other things, the Golden-Hardison interpretation of catharsis as "clarification" seems to have been determined by the following remarks in the *Poetics* : "Since the poet should provide pleasure from pity and fear through imitation, it is apparent that this function *must be worked into the incidents*" (italics added, XIV: 16-18). This remark has led them to relate catharsis to the *techne* of tragedy and to separate it from the *psychology of the audience.*

Similarly, despite their awareness of Aristotle's typically generic use of tragedy (cf "Aristotle did not consider tragedy from the modern point of view", p 113), they interpret tragedy in the specifically modern sense, i.e., in the sense of unhappy ending and advocate a necessary correlation between pitiable and fearful incidents, on the one hand, and tragedy, on the other. Their interpretation of catharsis as *tragic pleasure* (in the narrow sense, not in the Aristotelian sense) seems to have been determined by the following statement:

"We should not seek every pleasure from tragedy, but *only the one proper* to it" (italics added, *Poetics,* XIV: 13-15).

The theory of clarification is definitely the most attractive theory of catharsis in a comparative scheme of available interpretations. But it is not entirely free from certain disturbing limitations. It is not very difficult to show that this theory has its own share of lacunae, both terminological and interpretive, by pointing out some of the arguments used by the advocates of the theory themselves.

(i) First of all, the Golden-Hardison theory deserves to be criticized for its theoretical confusion. It sets up an unwarranted dichotomy between what it calls the *techne* of tragedy and the *psychology* of the audience. Aristotle does not merely talk about pity and fear being "worked into the incidents" of the plot; he also speaks of the "emotional effect", the "goal", the "artistic effect", and the "end" of tragic imitation (cf chapters XIV: 16-18, XIII: 24 & XXVI: 37-58). Tragedy has both a structure and a function and it performs its function only through its structure. Of course, the structure refers to the artist, and the function to the audience. But one cannot really separate the structure from the function or vice versa nor can one assign the function to the *techne*, independent of the psychology of the audience. The misplaced emphasis of the clarification theory on the techne of tragedy takes it to the other extreme of the same position that I A Richards took when he confined synthesis to the response of the reader. Catharsis, at once, refers both to the poet and to the audience, and, as the final cause of tragedy, it is the only link, the solitary meeting point between the technical expert and the connoisseurs of his art.

The authors of the clarification theory translate the catharsis clause as follows: "(Tragedy) achieves, through the representation of pitiable and fearful incidents, the catharsis of such pitiable and fearful incidents" (p 114) and contrast it with the following rendition of the clause (already quoted) by Ingram Bywater: "With incidents arousing pity and fear, wherewith to accomplish its Catharsis of such emotions". Defending their own version of the clause, the authors point out that their translation relates Catharsis to what happens in the tragedy itself, while Bywater's translation relates it to the psychology of the spectator (cf p 116). The view taken in this write-up is that catharsis illuminates the spectator's emotions by illuminating the incidents of the plot. It is worth noting here that emotions like pity and fear are associated with incidents in the sense in which action is associated with plot. Like plot, "incident" is part of the technical vocabulary of the techne of tragedy while pity and fear, like action, refer to the mode of our being, life as it is. What is action in life becomes plot in tragedy; likewise, what is pity or fear, happiness or misery, sanity or madness, in life, takes the form of an "incident" in the plot. Plot is an objectification of action; similarly, incidents are the artistic representation of emotions like pity and fear, happiness and misery. "A plot", says, Aristotle, "is a unity", and since "it is an imitation of an action, [it] must be an imitation of an action that is one and whole" (VIII: 1821-22). Emotions like pity and fear are parts which constitute the whole called action, and, as plot is an artistic analogue of action and a unity, incidents are the parts that constitute this unity. Catharsis is thus related to both. Art is not the work of a solitary genius who is bemused with his solitude; it is the work of a genius who is a rational and responsible, social human being who loves his humanity. Art is not only a creation; it is also a co-operating, a sharing and, the artist matters to his fellow human beings only because he shares his joys and sorrows with them. Aristotle's view of Catharsis cannot be alleged to have created a schism between the audience and the work of art.

(ii) The clarification theory does not attempt any explanation of Aristotle's apparently contrary remarks on tragedy. It does not, for example, show how Aristotle's definition of tragedy includes both *Oedipus* and *Iphigenia* as the best examples of tragedy nor does it account for the similarity or difference between the two occurrences of catharsis.

(iii) The third difficulty with the theory of Golden and Hardison is concerned with the choice of the term "clarification". Clarification does not adequately convey the full meaning of Aristotle's catharsis. But before we attempt to determine the meaning of catharsis with reference to the other terms associated with it, it is useful to have before us the relevant extracts from the *Poetics:*

(a) Tragedy achieves, through the representation of pitiable and fearful incidents, the *catharsis* of such pitiable and fearful incidents (VI: 9-11).

(b) The episodes must be appropriate, as, for example, the madness of Orestes through which he was captured and his deliverance through catharsis (XVII: 40-43).

(c) Tragedy in accomplishing its artistic effect, i.e., pleasure, is superior to epic (XXVI: 54-58).

(d) ... the poet should provide pleasure from pity and fear

through imitation (XIV: 16-17).

(e) The most effective recognition is one that occurs together with reversal .... For such a recognition will evoke pity or fear, and we have defined tragedy as an imitation of action of this type; and furthermore, happiness and misery will appear in circumstances of this type (XI: 13-14 & 21-24).

(f) ... a plot would be in accordance with pure human sympathy (XIII: 18-19).

(g) To give a general rule, we say that whatever length is required for a change to occur from bad fortune to good or from good fortune to bad through a series of incidents that are in accordance with probability or necessity, is a sufficient limit of magnitude (VII: 43-47).

(h) ... poetry is more concerned with the universal, and history more with the individual (IX: 13-14).

(i) ... tragedy exerts an influence on the soul (VI: 73-74).

(j) ... tragedy is an imitation of human action and life and happiness and misery (VI: 48-49).

(k) ... all men find pleasure in imitations. The proof of this point is what actually happens in life, for there are some things that distress us when we see them in reality, but the most accurate representations of the same things we view with pleasure — as, for example, the forms of the most despised animals and of corpses. The cause of this is that the act of learning is not only most pleasant to philosophers but, in a similar way, to other men as well. Thus men find pleasure in viewing representations because it turns out that they learn and infer what each thing is, for example, that this particular object is that kind of object... (men) will not find pleasure in the imitation *qua* imitation but rather in the workmanship (IV: 6-19).

Apart from giving valuable clues about what Aristotle probably meant by 'catharsis', these observations help us deduce certain generalizations regarding art in general and 'serious' drama in particular. Some of the generalizations could be like the following:

(i) Art converts the unconnected and the unintelligible into a pattern and thereby makes it intelligible. The artistic process is a process of universalization in two senses: it not only transforms multeity into a unity, it makes the particular and the local into something in which every soul finds an echo. The process of universalization operates "in accordance with the law of probability or necessity" and thus elicits "our human sympathy", our imaginative identity.

(ii) Life is painful and ugly but art is always pleasurable. The ordinary man's experience is chaotic but an aesthetic experience is a harmonious whole in which the parts not only have combined but have lost their separate identities. The artist, says Eliot (1953), possesses a sensibility "which can devour any kind of experience", the poet's mind is "constantly amalgating disperate experience. An ordinary man falls in love, or reads Spinoza, and these two experiences have nothing to do with each other, or with the noise of the typewriter or the smell of cooking, in the mind of the poet these experiences are always forming new wholes" (Eliot 1953). It is because of the poet's skill, his "workmanship", that an artistic imitation attains its beauty and delightfulness.

(iii) The aim, purpose, or function of a dramatic representation, as of all artistic representations, is to give pleasure to the audience (or the reader). Art pleases us by giving a unified vision of an integrated insight into reality and the unified vision is a perception or a discovery of the interconnection among apparently unrelated parts of reality. Art is not only a structure; it is also a vision, and the twin ingredients of structure and vision give aesthetic pleasure a unique status in the hierarchy of human experiences.

It was pointed out at the beginning of this write-up that in the Aristotelian scheme a phenomenon is believed to be the result of an interaction among four causes. It is possible, at least, in the sense of a mental abstraction, to categorize these four causes into two groups. The first three causes can be said to constitute a group, which for want of a better term, might be called "form" for the purposes of the present discussion, and the last will constitute a single-item-group which might (again, for want of a better term), be called "function". Having this distinction between form and function, we might relate catharsis and its equivalents to the latter and items like pity and fear, happiness and misery, madness and capture of Orestes, etc to the former. It will be obvious from this discussion that 'form' is used here in a fairly broad sense so as to subsume content, art and the relationship between the two. It is through the mediation of craftsmanship that content is changed into a work of art. Now, items like pity and fear certainly belong to that aspect of form which we call "content" here. But it is crucial to the understanding of Aristotle's concept of tragedy to realize that pity and fear are illustrative rather than exhaustive emotions. A critical reading of the *Poetics* does not support an unqualified equation between these emotions and what Aristotle meant by tragedy. Pity and fear refer to the necessity of conflict for drama. Drama deals with the basic contradictions of life, contradictions which are so deep-rooted and pervasive. Pity and fear, like happiness and misery, madness and sanity, light and darkness, good and evil, etc, are the two ends of the spectrum of dramatic conflict. Since Aristotle uses tragedy in the typical Greek sense of the word, the end of a play in terms of happiness or unhappiness need not be considered a determining factor for defining tragedy. Whether the end is fatal or fortunate, a tragedy is important because (like other forms of great art) it achieves a unity of effect, a resolution. Tragedy deals with tension and duality, confusion and contradiction, but the end-result is always an integrated vision, an insight. It is not for nothing that in its second and last occurrence in chapter XVII of the *Poetics*, catharsis is associated with "deliverance" and is contrasted with "capture" which follows "madness". Incidentally, this chapter also cites *Iphigenia in Tauris* to illustrate Aristotle's concept of the "universal form" of tragedy. Tragedy deals with "madness" but achieves, as its end, "deliverance" or liberation. Madness here clearly refers to the content of drama while deliverance to its artistic effect.

By relating catharsis to the function of drama, it is easy to see that it is associated with pleasure. Catharsis is Aristotle's technical term for the aesthetic pleasure produced by tragedy. This pleasure is an "act of learning" and learning emanates from the perception of the relationship between the "individual" and the "universal". Catharsis thus means "illumination". The translation of catharsis as illumination is endorsed by what Golden and Hardison themselves say, though they do not explicitly state this. Aristotle's theory of catharsis, they argue "is perhaps related to such contemporary aesthetic theories as James Joyce's idea of art as epiphany, a sudden, luminous perception of a previously hidden set of relations; to Benedetto Croce's experience of "coherence", and to the Jungian view of the aesthetic experience as a sudden "insight" into the archetypal forms of experience. All these doctrines share with Aristotle the notion of art as learning and the notion of learning as "pleasure" (p 295). This comparison between catharsis and illumination also makes catharsis a general theory of aesthetic experience.

However, the view finally taken in this article is that though Aristotle's theory of Catharsis is integral to his general theory of tragedy, it may very well be applied to literature in general, even to art, i.e., great art, in general. Aristotle probably meant that, of all the developed forms of art in his age, tragedy could achieve catharsis most effectively.

To sum up this part of the discussion, one more generalization needs to be made. The *Poetics* presents a theoretical framework in which imitative art, i.e., fine art, manifests itself at three levels: fine art in general, literature in general, and tragedy, i.e., serious drama, in general. It seems theoretically valid and logically sound to visualize this triple-manifestation of art in terms of three concentric circles, circles which have the same luminous centre. Taking Catharsis or *illuminative pleasure* as the centre, the circles can be distinguished only in that they have different radii. As concentric circles, they do not cut across one another, though they exist simultaneously and share a common centre. It is simply a matter of procedural choice whether one begins with the largest (the most general) and comes to the smallest (the most specific) or vice versa. Since Aristotle chooses to do the former, it is perfectly legitimate to say that within the Aristotelian framework tragedy offers the most concentrated variety of what we have called 'illuminative pleasure'. We might close this part with the following apology:

"Aristotle merely uses the term (Katharsis) without defining it ... and the question of what he actually meant is a *cause' celebre'* in the history of literary criticism. In so far there is no agreement yet, and none in sight, all definitions, including this one, must be regarded as definitions only" (Wheelwright 1965).

**4. Intersections between Rasa and Catharsis**

The present study is an attempt to bring out as many parallels as possible between the Aristotelian and the Bharatiya theories of drama. This does not, however, lead to any conjecture about a possible or actual historical connection between them. As a matter of fact, it is an emphatic denial of a mutual borrowing or influence of the *Poetics* on the *Natyashastra* or vice versa. The independent development of the two theories seems to be a fact which cannot be falsified or weakened on the basis of present scholarship. The complex of parallels between the two approaches that this study projects is just a matter of coincidence. Perhaps, it is literally true to say that great men always think alike. The numerous similarities between the theories of Aristotle and Bharata offer a concrete evidence of the mysterious meeting of minds across the barriers of time, place, language and culture.

4.1 The specific aim of this study is to identify and analyse all the possible intersections between the theories of Rasa and Catharsis, but it also has a few subsidiary concerns. One of such concerns is to show that there is an interesting parallel between Bharata's "Natya" and Aristotle's "Tragedy", for, both of them refer to a category of literary writings which, to borrow a phrase from Waith (1972), might be called "serious drama". There is, of course, an obvious antonymy between tragedy and comedy even within the *Poetics* but it must not be equated or confused with the modern antonymy between them. The classical Greek separation of comedy from tragedy necessitates a redefinition of our contemporary separation between them. Comedy for Aristotle means a play which deals with the frivolous, and, is witty and licentious. It evokes laughter which is opposed to tragic catharsis. Comedy is a "reverse or grotesque of serious poetry" (cf Wimsatt & Brooks 1964: 45) in many ways. As it deals with a much shorter canvas and offers only a tickle, it is consigned to a street-corner-sort of treatment in the *Poetics*. As it falls far short of the Aristotelian standard of a serious play, both in its treatment of life and its artistic effect, it is kept out of the general poetics of the drama. A serious play, Aristotle seems to have believed, must be informed by magnanimity, grandeur and sublimity. Such a play must be pervaded by some sort of heroic ethos, greatness of mind and largeness of heart. It must be an imitation of "nobility" on different levels and in different dimensions. It is eminently plausible to hypothesize that tragedy for Aristotle means that category of drama to which the great plays of Shakespeare, for example, belong, irrespective of whether they are tragedies, comedies, tragicomedies, or romances. It is this category of drama that Bharata describes as the quintessence of all knowledge, skill and art. The Bharatiya model of drama shares a common ground with the Aristotelian model to a much greater extent than could ordinarily be expected, though this generalization must not be seen as an unqualified equation between Bharata's "drama" and Aristotle's "tragedy". To appreciate the central thought of the argument presented in this study one must constantly remain conscious of the basic gap between the Indian and the Greek views of life, of their cultures.

It is possible to argue that the broad similarities between Aristotle's and Bharata's thoughts on drama arise from the thematic similarity between the two treatises. Besides, the point that really strikes the reader is that the *Poetics* and the *Natyashastra* not only deal with the same subject matter; surprisingly enough, they also adopt somewhat similar approaches to what they deal with. Each of them treats of drama in terms of four components, which, in this study are called matter, means, manner and function. Analysing the parallels with reference to these components, it is of the greatest significance to note that both Aristotle and Bharata define drama as "an imitation of human action". It is highly probable that the correspondences between the theories on the language, manner, and function of drama follow from this basic conceptual identity. Many of the theoretical constructs are common to both approaches.

4.2 If the respective surveys of views on Rasa and Catharsis are compared, it should not be difficult to see that there are a number of intersections between the two concepts. It is not only that the Rasasutra occurs in the sixth chapter of the *Natyashastra* as the catharsis clause occurs in the sixth chapter of the *Poetics*; the Rasasutra, like the catharsis clause, has been one of the most controversial maxims in the history of poetics. The correspondence between the terms, i.e., Rasasutra and Catharsis clause, is too obvious to need any explanation. One could without much detriment to terminological clarity, interchange clause with sutra and use phrases like the Rasa clause or the Catharsis sutra. Each of them is a formula. Each of these formulas contains an inscrutable gap or lacuna, no one knows, whether by accident or design. Aristotle does not define Catharsis, while Bharata does not include *sthayibhava* (dominant emotion) in his formulation of the process of Rasa-realization. Both Catharsis and Rasa share more or less the same number of schools of interpretation. Neither of these terms is a neologism; Rasa and Catharsis are picked up from the contemporary flow of language. But this does not in any way affect their status as technical terms. In their respective systems they turn out to be the nucleus of technical vocabulary.

4.3 The central point of the Rasa-Catharsis convergence is decidedly the doctrine of universalization. The transformation of the ordinary into the aesthetic, of the painful into the joyous and, above all, of the objective into the subjective is effected through the process of universalization. Besides, both the theory of Rasa and the theory of Catharsis distinguish aesthetic pleasure from mere sense-gratification, as also from transcendental meditation. Aesthetic pleasure is neither sensual nor spiritual, neither mundane nor celestial, neither indulgent nor mortifying; it is the wonderful "intermediate" and hence, it is *sui generis*. The aesthetic experience is at once a pleasure and an illumination. It is a pleasure because it is an illumination and, it is an illumination because it is a discovery or perception of the universal in the specific. It is on this triad of pleasure, illumination and perception of the universal-specific relationship that Rasa and Catharsis come closest to each other and it is here that they share a kind of fraternity which is generally overlooked.

4.4 This Rasa-Catharsis fraternity, however, may give rise to two more questions. The first of these questions could be: Is aesthetic pleasure a feature of the stimulating object, the work of art, or is it an experience of the spectator (or reader)? With the surveys of the theories of Rasa and Catharsis in mind, one could point out that in both traditions aesthetic pleasure has been assigned sometimes to the work and sometimes to the spectator's experience. Lollatta and Shankuka in case of Rasa, and, Golden and Hardison in case of Catharsis, have advocated theories which consider aesthetic pleasure an objective identity, while certain other scholars, *viz.*, Nayak and Abhinava in India, and Richards in the West), take it to be a subjective entity, an experience of the spectator. The view taken in the present study is that aesthetic pleasure (as indicated by Rasa and Catharsis) is both an objective as well as a subjective entity. It is at once a feature of a work of art and an experience of the spectator. Aesthetic pleasure draws its life from the work of art but it acquires its meaning only when it finds its way into the heart of the *sahirdaya* (or the spectator).

The second question arising out of the Rasa-Catharsis intersection could be: Does Aristotle suggest several types of Catharsis as Bharata does in the case of Rasa? The answer is: perhaps, yes. On the basis of our own experience of witnessing plays (or even other works of art) we can say that we do not get the same kind of pleasure from all plays. It is not only that plays differ in their effect on the audience in keeping with their having a happy or unhappy ending; *Oedipus* and *Iphigenia* certainly differ in their artistic effect. But, more importantly, we realize that even two tragedies differ from each other in their effects. *Macbeth* cannot be said to achieve the same effect on the audience as *Hamlet* does and it is not a question of discussing a play as better than or worse than another. All great plays, like other great works of art, produce aesthetic pleasure (whether Rasa or Catharsis) and yet two plays can be distinguished from each other in respect of their producing two different types of aesthetic pleasure. This sort of differentiation, however, is describable in terms of the dominant emotion that a particular play develops and evokes. The variety of aesthetic pleasure derivable from *Macbeth* as different from the one derivable from *Hamlet* can best be described with reference to their respective dominant emotions (*sthayibhavas*). Aristotle seems to indicate two types of aesthetic pleasure when he mentions plays like *Oedipus* and *Iphigenia*. It is not really important from the point of view of constructing a theory of drama whether Aristotle suggests two types of pleasure or more. What really matters is the fact that the Aristotelian framework recognizes the possibility of differentiation in aesthetic pleasure. As for the number of Rasas, it must be noted that there is no unanimity among scholars on this issue. Bharata mentions eight kinds of Rasa while later theorists raise this number to twelve (cf Mukherjee 1966: 317-335). It seems most plausible to take this classification as illustrative rather than as exhaustive. What brings Aristotle and Bharata closer to each other on this question is that there is, in each system, a recognition of differentiating plays from one another even with reference to the type of aesthetic pleasure that they provide. But the most important point of intersection between Rasa and Catharsis is that each of them is emphatic on the achievement of the artistic effect as the highest function of a dramatic representation whether it is *drama* in Bharata's sense or *tragedy* in the Aristotelian sense.

Now that the study has more than justified the choice of the title, it is only proper that further analysis of the correspondence between Catharsis and Rasa be left to future research.

# Auchitya and Decorum: Parallel Developments in Poetics

"First, never go against the best light you have; secondly, take care that your light be not darkness"

— Bishop Wilson cited in *Culture and Anarchy* (p 29)

No two ancient civilizations seem to share so many streams of thought and so many strands of 'culture' (in the Arnoldian sense) as do those of India and Greece. Whether we think of speculative philosophy or political theory, of political institutions or social organization, of mathematics or metaphysics, of educational planning or social ethics, or, of literature or the study of language, we do invariably discover some sort of an academic partnership between the thinkings of ancient India and ancient Greece. As the two major constituents of the Indo-Aryan family, as the intellectual leaders of mankind, as the first founders of institutionalized forms of education (from the primary to the university level) or as the earliest architects of the republican form of government, India and Greece would be found to have a genuine claim to many a first in several areas of human thinking and doing. The *Mahabharata* and the *Ramayana*, the *Iliad* and the *Odyssey*, the *Republic* and the *Arthashastra*, the *Poetics* and the *Natyashastra* are some of the earliest records of the sublimity of human knowledge and experience in a variety of domains. The most fascinating aspect of such an academic partnership or cultural fraternity between India and Greece lies in the fact that the two traditions of scholarship display a mutually agreed regard for the supremacy of the human intellect in every sphere of life. The *Dialogues* of Plato, like the great *Upanishads*, make it absolutely clear that the search for knowledge is the best use of human intelligence and the highest culture that the human race as a race can ever aspire to. In both, knowledge is the impelling motive of the interlocutors. In both, knowledge is regarded as an object of supreme value. In both, the idea of the worth and efficacy of knowledge is expressed again and again. For people in ancient India and Greece knowledge (both as means and end) was culture. *Culture*, Mathew Arnold tells us time and again in his matchless classic, 'is a pursuit of our total perfection by means of getting to know everything that most concern us; it is "a free play of intelligence on all things"; "or a disinterested endeavour to learn and propagate the best that is known and thought in the world". No country or race pursued *culture* on so many levels and in so many dimensions as did Hellenic philosophers and Upanashadic seers in those dark and difficult times (around 500 BC). It is in such a pursuit of complete culture that ancient India and ancient Greece come closer to each other than do any other pair of nations in the history of the ancient world.

**Similarities between Indo-Greek Literary Theories**

As there are a number of striking similarities between what the ancient Greeks and the ancient Indians thought and did, one could, with sufficient academic justification and without much difficulty, identify a number of areas which could be called 'Indo-Greek'. Thus, one could talk about Indo-Greek philosophy, literature, linguistics, polity, poetics and so on. But when a term like *Indo-Greek Poetics* is used, it must be clearly emphasized that the use of such terms does not assume any mutual borrowing or influence between the Greek and the Indian traditions of scholarship which, as far as we know, developed quite independently of each other. The term *Indo-*

*Greek Poetics* must not be intended to supersede the autonomy of terms like Greek poetics and Indian poetics nor to huddle up the one against the other in some sort of straitjacket. It should be used to refer to only those areas of theorizing about literature in which the two traditions of scholarship stand face to face with each other, whether to meet or to clash, whether to agree or to disagree, over a certain point of view. Indo-Greek poetics would therefore subsume within itself all the points of commonality between Indian poetics and Greek poetics whether these points refer to meetings or to clashes, to agreements or to disagreements. As soon as an area of literary theorizing happens to be common to both traditions, it can quite legitimately be taken as part of Indo-Greek poetics.

In the previous chapter I have tried to highlight certain striking similarities between the theories of Catharsis and Rasa with reference to the *Poetics* and the *Natyashastra*. The present chapter is an attempt to identify certain commonalities between *Auchitya* and *Decorum* with particular reference to the *Ars Poetica* of Horace and the *Auchitya-Vicharcharcha* of Kshemendra. It is an interesting exercise to discover and pinpoint those striking similarities which bring these two famous theories in Poetics so close to each other, although there is no evidence to suggest that there ever was any mutual borrowing or influence between Indians and Greeks in regard to the theory of propriety in literature.

## Role of Poetry

I would like to begin this analysis by posing two commonplace questions; questions which agitate all those who care about poetry (in the sense of literature or art in general) and about its relevance to human living; questions which have been asked and answered in many ages and in various parts of the human world; and, above all, questions which remain, to this day, as fresh and unnerving as they were during Plato's life time. These two questions are: (1) Why does poetry matter to us? and (2) How does poetry do what it does? Since it is extremely difficult, if not impossible, to be original about such matters, I would avail myself of the average educated man's privilege of reproducing what others have been saying for ages by way of answering these questions. When we ponder over the first question, we realize that poetry matters to us because it is a privilege peculiar to the human race, to *homo sapiens*. It matters to us because it does something which no other variant of human ingenuity can do. It occupies a unique position in the hierarchy of human acts and experiences by virtue of its innate capacity to fuse the mundane with the celestial, the specific with the universal, the temporal with the timeless, the necessary with the probable, and, the factual with the fantastic. It is through its unique capacity for such fusions that it relates human life, at a time, 'to the kindred points of heaven and home'. The greatness of poetry lies in its paradoxical nature and behaviour: it ties us down to the horrors of living as successfully as it launches us into those sublime heights of passionate living where ecstasy and illumination hold each other in an amorous embrace. Poetry is indispensable to human living in either case because it is an 'insight experience', 'an epiphany', 'a sudden and luminous perception' of a hidden set of relations in the intellective-cum-experiential domains of our existence (cf the previous chapter). Poetry matters to us also because it is the only secular human construct which sustains and energizes the Sattva component of our personality.

When we ponder over the second question, we realize that poetry is both a vision and a structure, an idea and an incarnation, an experience and an incantation, and, a function and a form. The vision, the idea, the experience, or the function is great. But so is the structure, the incarnation, the incantation or the form. Now, we have to bear in mind that it is only through the structure that the vision is formed and communicated. Poetry creates its magic effect on the reader/ listener/ viewer not because it contains experience but because it is a structured experience. We turn to poetry not to gain in wisdom nor to acquire importance; we turn to poetry because in it we discover a vision formed, an experience articulated, and, because each of such visions or experiences turns out to be the echo of every sensitive soul. Poetry achieves its unique effect or performs its unique function only through its structure or form. 'Form', it should be noted, is used here is its typical Aristotelian sense in which it is nearly synonymous with a work of art. In the Aristotelian system, as we all know, 'form' (as opposed to 'function') is, at once, shape and that which shapes, structure and that which structures, form and that which is formed: "Where there is form, there will be matter, *informed*, where there is matter, there will be form, informing" (LaDriere 1970). Now, the moment we think of the *form* of a work of art, we are constrained to take note of the network of relations in and around the work of art, relations that hold among the parts, between the parts and the whole, and between one whole and other wholes. When we take note of such relations within and around a work of art, we realize that there must be a frame of reference within which the work could be placed and analysed. Once we visualize the necessity of such a frame of reference to analyze the internal and external relations of a work of art, we are obliged to draw a distinction between what a work is and what it ought to be. This is the genesis of the normative/evaluative matrix of literary theory and criticism. Every normative/ evaluative theory of literature is essentially concerned with the problem of relatedness, whether of part to part, of parts to the whole, or of one whole to another whole. Every such theory is based on an implied sense of 'propriety', whether under this name or under any other. Some other names could be: fitness, symmetry, coherence, order, harmony, aptness, congruity, correctness, unity, keeping and appropriateness. It does not really matter which term we use. The choice of the term is just a matter of personal preference. Propriety is *prepon* in Greek, *Decorum* in Latin and *Auchitya* in Sanskrit. My choice of the pair of terms, 'Auchitya and Decorum', for the title of this chapter, does not imply any relative superiority of the one to the other nor does it suggest any duality between the two. The choice is meant only to suggest that these terms are equivalents and that one can easily pass from Auchitya to Decorum or from Decorum to Auchitya without causing any detriment to the principle of propriety in literature. The parallelism between these two theories offers another example of how two traditions of scholarship could do the same thing under different labels and without either of them having any knowledge of what the other had done or was doing.

## I

Decorum, as applied to literature, is generally defined as the appropriate rendering of situation, character, action and speech (cf Herrick 1965, Abrams 1978: 38 & Ency Brit 1980: 428). According to this theory, in a good literary work, action should fit situation and character, thought and feeling should fit character and situation, and expression should fit subject matter so that one can easily separate the lofty from the ludicrous (cf Herrick 1965). Decorum is often linked with internal harmony within the work, with harmony of *part to part* and of *parts to the whole* (Shipley 1970). Such a view of decorum relates it to the conception of beauty as "dependent on order and fitness" (Gilbert 1970). But since everything in the universe stands in some relation to other things, proponents of literary decorum generally tend to emphasize "the conformity of related things to one another" with reference to "a recognized ideal" (LaDriere 1970). As the theory of decorum always implies a sense of "established or accepted values", sensitivity to literary propriety or correctness varies from age to age and is likely to be greater when and where "the observance of formal conventions is felt to be important" (Palmer 1973). We can therefore easily account for shifts in emphasis on the essentiality or significance of adherence to the theory of decorum from time to time.

The evolution of the theory of decorum has passed through a long and chequered history from the fourth century BC to our own times. Some of the notable figures associated with this history have been: Aristotle, Cicero, Horace, Giraldi Cinthio, Puttenham, Sidney, Milton, Addison, Goldsmith, Johnson, Coleridge, Bridges and Spingarn.

**Literary decorum**

The concept of literary decorum was outlined by Aristotle in the *Rhetoric* and the *Poetics*. Aristotle uses terms like *Prepon*, *prepousa* and *harmotton* to define appropriateness in style and characterization in dramatic writings (cf Herrick 1965 & Gilbert 1970). "Style to be good", Aristotle remarks in the *Rhetoric* (1404[b]), "must be clear, as is proved by the fact that speech which fails to convey a plain meaning will fail to do just what speech has to do. It must also be appropriate, avoiding both manners and undue elevation". He goes on to say that elevation is quite *fitting* in poetry because "things there spoken of are comparatively remote from ordinary life" but such elevation will be far less fitting in prose passages because "the subject matter is less exalted". A little later (1408[a]), Aristotle observes: "Your language will be *appropriate* if it expresses emotion and character, and if it corresponds to the subject". Explaining the meaning of *correspondence* he adds: "We must neither speak casually about weighty matters, nor solemnly about trivial ones".

According to Aristotle, it is obligatory for the dramatist to ensure that appropriateness is observed at various levels: plot, character, diction and spectacle. He argues that in "constructing plots and working them out with diction, the poet must keep the action as much as possible before his eyes. For by *visualizing* the events as distinctly as he can, just as if he were present at their actual occurrence, he will discover what is *fitting* for his purpose and there will be the least chance of incongruities escaping his notice" (*Poetics* XVII: 1-6, italics added). As plot is directly related to diction because the episodes are ultimately worked out through written speeches, the dramatist cannot avoid being particular about the suitability of diction to character and situation. Aristotle also demands that character "must be appropriate" (XV: 9). It is not proper, he says, for a man to be *unmanly* or for a woman to be *manly* (XV: 10-12). Here Aristotle seems to be thinking of the assignment of type characteristics to characters in a play in terms of their sex, age, social class, profession and nationality (cf Hardison 1968: 202). Similarly, he requires spectacle to be *fitting* and free from incongruities. Here again he says that because of its technical constraints, tragedy cannot admit as much of the *marvellous* as epic can (XXIV: 57-64).

Cicero, the peerless artist of the spoken word, defines decorum in its general application to real life, oratory and poetry. "For as in life", says Cicero (the *Orator* 70), "so in art, nothing is harder than to see what is fit" (cited in LaDriere 1970). One of the interlocutors—Crassus—observes in *On the Orator* (32), the best known of Cicero's works: "I had heard ... lectures on the traditional rules for the embellishment of style in connection with which the first requirement is pure and good Latin, the second clearness and lucidity, the third artistic finish, the fourth suitability to the subject and a certain elegance of form" (Hadas 1951: 215). In the *Orator* (II, III: 9-10, 12) Cicero says: "Whatever topic a person undertakes to discuss rationally and methodically, he ought to reduce it to its ultimate and proper character and form" (cited in Wimsatt and Brooks 1964: 81).

**Three Unique Personalities**

Aristotle, Cicero and Horace are generally regarded as the three "leading arbiters of poetic decorum" but it is Horace whose theory of decorum is best known through his famous *Ars Poetica*. The central argument of this book is concerned with literary propriety and the favourite passage runs between lines 89 and 127, wherein the poet tells us that each style must keep its proper place. It was due to these lines that

Horace became the most remarkable figure of the later classical period and could exercise so much influence on subsequent critical thinking, particularly on the criticism and practice of literature in the Renaissance and the Neo-Classical Age (cf Abrams 1978: 38). The *Ars Poetica* is perhaps the single ancient poem on poetics, perhaps the solitary ancient poem which insists that writing poetry is a responsible exercise governed by a set of well-defined rules. The counter-argument that a poet feels cramped and confined by his chosen theme, situation, character or metre is like suggesting that a "squash-player feels restricted by the walls of his court" (Rudd 1973). As a versified essay on literary criticism, the *Ars poetica* is easily reducible to a finite set of precepts the adherence to which is essential to the writing of great poetry. A modern critic divides the 476 lines of the poem into 29 precepts most of which he finds *sensible enough* and rooted in Aristotle's works on literary criticism (cf Wilkinson 1968: 98-100). Does the Horatian theory of decorum refer to something intrinsic to the nature of things or to something established by human convention? The critical assumptions of Horace take the middle way which stands for "a thorough inter-penetration of nature and convention in the classical literary tradition" (Wimsatt & Brooks 1964: 83). In a wider sense, Horace does define the idiom of all poetry. As Eliot puts it:

> "The word neither diffident nor ostentatious,
> An easy commerce of the old and the new,
> The common word exact without vulgarity,
> The formal word precise but not pedantic".
>
> (*Little Gidding* V: 5-9)

Horace draws a comprehensive framework of literary decorum which demands the choice of appropriate theme, proper diction, suitable character types and a clear view of structural unity or wholeness. A writer who violates the principle of structural wholeness is like a man who paints "a dolphin in a forest" or "a wild boar in the waves". The choice of the proper theme enhances the writer's felicity of expression. The choice of diction must be in conformity with the subject matter; "a comic subject cannot be presented in tragic verse nor tragic subjects can be presented in comic verse". Words must match the moods they describe; "sad words suit a gloomy countenance, menacing words angry; sportive words a merry look, stern words a grim look". Similarly, words must be appropriate to the speaker in terms of his age, status, sex, profession, nationality, etc. The writer must also pay careful attention to the type traits of his characters; the child goes one way, the adult another, and the old man still another. It is a gross violation of decorum to assign an old man's part to a youth or a man's part to a woman.

Horace's insistence on the observance of propriety in various respects does not, however, blind him to the desirability of a writer's freedom. The Horatian dictum is a fine synthesis of freedom and restraint:

"Painters and poets alike have always enjoyed the right to take what risks they please;

I know; I grant that freedom but not to the point of allowing wild to couple with tame, or showing a snake and a bird, a lamb and a tiger, as partners".

The idea of decorum passed into the Renaissance as the all-embracing critical doctrine. Giraldi Cinthio writes: "Decorum is nothing other than grace and fitness of things, and should be thought of not merely as to actions but to speech and reply between men. Nor should this be considered only in the work as a whole, but in every part of it" (cited in Gilbert 1970). Puttenham does not accept any rigidity about the principle of decorum; it is not a matter of weak and ignorant judgement; rather it "resteth in the discerning part of the mind" (cited in Palmer 1973). Puttenham's term is *decencie*. As a concept it is quite flexible and open-ended: "this *decencie* comes to be very much alterable and subject to *varietie* in so much as our speech asketh one manner of *decencie* in respect of the person who speaks, another of him to whom it is spoken, another of what we speak, and in what place and time and to what purpose" (cited in LaDriere 1970). Philip Sidney, like Puttenham, uses *decency* to mean decorum. The Horatian dictum is quite evident in Sidney's pronounced contempt for the mingling of tragedy and comedy, "the mongrel tragi-comedy" (1975: 400). Such mingling, Sidney believed, violated the principle of dramatic 'decency'.

By the seventeenth century decorum came to achieve a highly elaborate form in literary theory and practice. As interpreted by critics and commentators, decorum called for "distinct poetic genres, consistent characters and the careful observance of the classical hierarchy of styles: grand, moderate and plain" (Herrick 1965). The authority of a poet like Milton gave the doctrine a reputation and acceptability it had seldom claimed before. In his *Tractate of Education,* Milton spoke of the crowning study of poetry as "that sublime art which in Aristotle's *Poetics,* in Horace, and in the Italian commentaries of Castelvetro, Tasso, Mazzoni and others, teaches what the laws are of a true epic poem, what of a dramatic, what of lyric, what *decorum* is, which is the grand *masterpiece to observe*" (Milton 637, italics added). The neo-classical period discovered in the *Ars Poetica* the main inspiration for their standards of *correctness* and norms of *elegance.* Elegance and correctness stood for literary propriety, for a propriety that avoided the vulgar as well as the unconventional. The Augustans were not prepared to tolerate any deviation from the norm set by convention and common sense. Oliver Goldsmith, for example, held: "What must be the entire perversion of scenical decorum, when, for instance, we see an actress ... unwieldy with fat endeavoring to convince the audience that she is dying with hunger" (cited in Gilbert 1970). Addison found fault with the form of the conversation between Adam and Eve in *Paradise Lost* as it violated, in his view, the sense of propriety: "Milton makes Adam speak the most endearing things without descending from his natural dignity, and the woman receiving them without departing from the modesty of her character" (cited *ibid*). By the critical canons of neo-classicism, decorum regulated the distinction between literary genres, determining what kind of style and subjectmatter were in keeping with each other. Neo-classicists like Dryden, Pope and Johnson consistently charge Shakespeare with having mixed up tragedy with comedy and high style with low style (cf Palmer 1973). Even Coleridge advocated a neat separation of literary genres and styles: "No sensible poet or critic can quibble very much with the admonition that it is unseemly to use high-sounding expressions when speaking of the gutter and equally unseemly to use mean expressions when speaking of the majesty of Rome" (cited in Herrick 1965).

At this stage of our account, it is significant to note that too much insistence on the mechanical observance of propriety, whether in respect of subjectmatter or style, situations or character types, literary genres or modes of writing, might lead to a kind of literalism which will militate against the very nature and function of literary creativity. Distinctions in literature, like those in life, can never be absolute and eternal. We have to make allowances for variations/deviations in every aspect of literary activity. The vagaries of Shakespeare's critical reputation illustrate how the principle of decorum could atrophy the critical activity of the great Augustans. This enables us to better appreciate why writers who radically depart from accepted conventions are considered indecorous by their contemporaries. The contemporary critical reactions to poets like Shakespeare, Donne, Wordsworth and Eliot (to take only a few examples) point to the severe limitations of critical criteria based on the mechanical application of the rules/precepts of decorum. When we have cases like these before us, we realize that there is something basically wrong with such critical criteria. We are therefore obliged to take the view that "the sense of decorum lies not in the rigid prescription of absolute laws but in a tactful and flexible judgement"(Palmer 1973). It is in this context that we come to appreciate critics like Robert Bridges and J E Spingarn. Robert Bridges, in his well-known essay on `Poetic Diction' (1933), uses terms like *Property* and *Keeping* (borrowed from stage and painting respectively) to point out the essential purpose of decorum. He points out that in aesthetics no property can be taken as absolutely good or bad: "Different properties are indispensable for different imaginative effects". Everything depends on "where" and"how" it is used. Bridges does not agree either with Johnson or with Wordsworth because both of them tend to label certain absurdities and excellences as absolutes. Bridges, on the contrary, holds the view that "good keeping is a first essential in all good writing, and especially in poetry" and therefore, "no property is absurd if it is in keeping". Like Bridges, Spingarn is of the view that poetic flaws and excellences are never absolute; they are always relative. As he puts it: "It is inconceivable that a modern thinker should still adhere to the abstract tests of good expression, when it is obvious that we can only tell whether it is good or bad when we see it in its neutral context" (cited in Raghavan 1970).

## II

### Theory of Auchitya

The history of Indian thinking on Auchitya as one of the central concerns of literary theory and criticism begins with the *Natyashastra*, the earliest and the most authoritative treatise on poetics, sometimes believed to have been written in the fifth century BC (cf Shastri 1972: 93). We do not come across any remarkable work on Auchitya during the lean period of Indian poetics between Bharata and Bhamah, i.e., from the second half of the fifth century BC to the end of the first half of the seventh century AD). But we do find a number of books dealing with Auchitya, in one way or another, from the second half of the seventh century to the end of the eleventh. The galaxy of theorists like Bhamah, Yashovarman, Vaman, Dandin, Anandavardhana, Rudrata, Kuntaka, Mahimabhatta, Abhinavagupta and Kshemendra, who together constitute the *golden age* of Sanskrit poetics, do come up one after another with a great variety of insightful remarks by way of refining and elaborating the theory of Auchitya with the result that at the end of the eleventh century Auchitya is firmly established as a venerable member of the critical trinity, the other two being Rasa and Dhvani. Looking back, we discover that in its long and historic march from Bharata to Kshemendra, Auchitya undergoes several stages of theoretical sophistication so that ultimately it turns out to be a sufficiently flexible and definitive frame of reference for the determination of quality in literature. The theory of Auchitya contains a set of critical criteria which enables us to separate the good from the bad or the remarkable from the useless in literature, whether we consider the different parts of a work or different works.

To our understanding of the theory of Auchitya as presented in the *Natyashastra* of Bharata, two sets of distinctions are very important. The first set consists of regional/racial characteristics of human nature versus the universals of human nature, i.e., *Pravriti* vs *Prakriti*, while the second set consists of conformity to the ways of the world versus conformity to accepted values and conventions in literature, i.e., *Lokadharmee* vs *Natyadharmee* cf NS 6: 24, 14: 71-82 & 23: 191). Prakriti, Pravriti, Lokadharma and Natyadharma could easily be taken as the general determinants of literary propriety. When we consider a work of art, we should, for example, first find out if the work (or any of its parts) is in keeping with some or all of these determinants. A work of art to be acceptable has to conform either to some literary convention or to the facts of life or to both. Similarly, a work has to depict human nature in general or the regional/racial characteristics of human nature or both. In either case, the work has to be referred to something outside of itself. Conformity is a relational concept. Any judgement of a literary work from the point of view of Auchitya involves reference to a norm which is different from and independent of the work being judged. Bharata seems to be absolutely clear about this assumption whenever he discusses the norms of judging a successful play. His view of Auchitya seems to be very comprehensive: it ranges from the suitability of theme, characterization and dialogue to that of stage management, costume-designing and make-up. As drama is a representation of situations, moods and ways of life, it becomes significant to find out whether there is an appropriateness of representation in respect of variables like action, character, dialogue, dress, spectacle and so on. Whether he discusses the flaws and excellences of poetry (*Kavyadosha* and *Kavyaguna* as in chapter 17) or speech varieties to be used by and for characters (as in chapters 18-19) or the relationship between the figures of speech and the varying moods or sentiments of characters (as in chapter 17) or dress and make-up (as in chapter 23), Bharata always seeks to point out what suits what. For him, as for many others, excellence or flaw does not inherently pertain to anything as such. A thing is either suitable or not in a particular situation and in this suitability or the lack of it lies excellence or flaw. A well-dressed woman is fully acceptable as a character in a play when she goes to meet her lover but it is highly improper for the dramatist (or the stage manager) to present a lady suffering separation from her lover as having her body fully decked with jewels (cf Raghavan 1970). Bharata further says that dress or ornament does not by itself "render the body charming unless worn at the proper place, as, for example, a girdle worn at the breast produces only laughter or ridicule:

*Adeshajo hi Veshastu nashobham janayishyati;*
*Mekhalorasi baddhatu hasyam samupapadyate"*

(NS 23: 70)

Whatever may be the specific requirements of Auchitya, Bharata makes it very clear that the general demand that a theory of literary propriety must meet is to make it obligatory for every dramatic work to conform to the truths of life:

*"Lokasiddham bhavet siddham natyam lokatmakam tatha,*
*Tasmannatya prayogo tu pramanam loka ishyate"*, i.e., since a play is a representation of human life, the only reference point

to judge its merit as a play is the way of the world" (NS 26: 126).

According to the late seventh century theorist, Bhamah, the greatest excellence of poetry lies in Auchitya, while the worst flaw of poetry lies in Anauchitya (indecorum). In chapter 4 of his *Kavyalankar* he says that the style must be appropriate to the literary genre and theme as also to the character and situation. There are no fixed flaws or excellences in poetry. All poetic flaws originate from the violation of Auchitya which is itself flexible. Depending on the context, Gunas become Doshas and vice versa. What is acceptable in one context becomes absurd in another and vice versa. "Redundance (*Punarukti*), for example, is generally a flaw in style but it becomes an excellence if it is used to express feelings of fear, sorrow or jealousy" (*Kavyalankar* 4: 14).

In the first half of the eighth century, King Yashovarman of Kannauj used the word *Auchitya* for the first time in his play *Ramabhyudaya*. He mentions two kinds of Auchitya: Auchitya of expression and Auchitya of context. According to the first, the dramatist is urged to prepare his dialogue suitable to the nature and rank of his characters while, according to the second, the dramatist is required to delineate his characters in their proper moods so as to develop proper Rasa (cf Raghavan 1970).

To Vamana Auchitya means propriety in the use of language. His only criterion to identify a statement as appropriate or inappropriate is to test it against commonsense. He points out in his *kavyalankarsutra* that statements in poetry which violate the appropriateness of time, place and ordinary experience are undesirable because they are at variance with commonsense:

*Deshakalasvabhava viruddharthani lokaviddha* (2, 2: 23)

This is closely paralleled by the following remark of Dandin in his *Kavyadarsha*:

*Kantam sarvajagat kantam laukikarthanatikramati*, i.e., poetry which does not violate the truth of ordinary experience, pleases all and is therefore the best poetry" (1: 85).

Dandin holds, like Bhamah, that poetic flaws and excellences are not absolutes or constants. Flaws like meaninglessness, contradiction and redundance cease to be so and even become excellences when they describe states of mind which call for such expressions. If a poet were to describe a madman's raving, a child's prattle, or the speech of a very sick man, such expressions are eminently justified and proper (cf 3: 128-141).

Anandavardhana renders the relativity between flaws and excellences more explicit when he posits that flaws and excellences in poetry are contingent (*anitya*) and that there are no independent flaws and excellences. We must note that in the history of Sanskrit poetics Anandavardhana is the first critic to mention Auchitya as one of the *essentials* of poetry (Raghavan 1970). He discusses three main varieties of Auchitya: the Auchitya of language, the Auchitya of subjectmatter and the Auchitya of characterization. He is of the view that the greatest function of poetry is the manifestation of Rasa and that the real secret of Rasa-manifestation is Auchitya:

*Anauchityadrite nanyadrasabhangasya karanam,*
*Prasiddhauchityabandhastu rasasyopanishatpara*

*i.e.,* there is no other cause for a breach in Rasa except indecorum. The greatest secret about Rasa is conformity to well-known considerations of decorum" (*Dhvanyaloka* 3: 14).

It was left to the eminent theorist of the later half of the ninth century, named Rudrata, to establish Auchitya as a technical term in poetics. He uses Auchitya as a technical term in his discussion of Alankara in chapter 2 of his *Kavyalankara*. Beyond this, Rudrata does not make any significant contribution to the development of the theory of Auchitya. His arguments in favour of the adherence to Auchitya in poetry are more or less a repetition of what his predecessors have already said. He says, for example, that since drama is an imitation of life, the dramatist must depict an infinite variety of people and situations all of which must conform to real-life people and situations. Whatever conforms to the ways of the world is appropriate. Similarly, he points out that decorum depends on what suits the context. When a madman, for example, is being represented, his nonsense will have to be represented. This nonsense becomes *sense* for the dramatist. Whatever suits a context is proper and what does not fit in with the context is incongruous:

*Yadanuchitam yatra tattatraivopajayate gramyam*, i.e., a word becomes awkward (gramya) if it does not agree with the context (6: 17).

According to Kuntaka, a tenth century theorist, Auchitya is nearly synonymous with proper expression. He agrees that the poet's main task is the successful depiction of the theme or Rasa and that Auchitya should be judged with reference to the poet's success in performing this task but he clearly holds that the best proof of Auchitya lies in the strikingness of expressions. The very title of his book called *Vakrokti-Jivita* suggests his definition of Auchitya. However, he makes it quite explicit in the following verse:

*Anjanasena svabhavasya mahatvamyena poshyate,*

*Prakarena tadauchitya muchite khyanamajivitam* (1: 53) *i.e.*, that quality is known as 'propriety' by virtue of which the poetic expression gains in a most lucid manner; in fact it may be regarded as the vital essence of all poetic descriptions". Such strikingness of expression, Kuntaka believes, must be evident in every element of poetry like the word, the sentence and the work as a whole: *padavakaprabandhanam vyapakatvena vartate* (1: 57).

But to the greatest theorist in the post-Bharata history of Sanskrit poetics, Abhinavagupta of the early eleventh century, Auchitya is essential but not all important in poetry. It comes only after Rasa and Dhvani and, thus, occupies the third position in the hierarchy of the theories of literature. Besides, unlike Rasa, Auchitya is a means to an end. The end is the realization of Rasa and Auchitya is only a means to that end. Auchitya is a certain sort of relatedness among the parts of a work of art and as such it is quite important. But it cannot and must not replace Rasa as the central concern of literary activity. Abhinavagupta loudly declares that a critic who regards Auchitya as an end in itself does not understand the nature of literary creativity (cf Raghavan 1970).

The later half of the eleventh century, however, witnessed the final development of the theory of Auchitya in the work of a critic called Kshemendra who was perhaps the only writer on poetics to devote a full-length book to Auchitya. It is mainly due to the *Auchitya Vicharcharcha* that Auchitya became the third most important theory in Indian poetics. The most historic contribution of Kshemendra to the evolution of the theory of Auchitya lay in that he offered a systematic and exhaustive exposition of the concept and showed it to be the life of poetry (*Kavyajivita* cf Mukherji 1966: 23-25, Raghavan 1970 & Sankaran 1973: 146-47). He took the essentiality of Rasa for granted and posited that, as decorum constituted the very life of a poetic creation, it was indispensable to the realization of Rasa. His scheme of Auchitya is so comprehensive that it includes almost everything associated with creative activity. He mentions as many as 27 determinants of literary decorum in his work (verses 8-10). Some of the main determinants are: time, place, profession, family background, age, class, real-life situations, human nature, subjectmatter, purpose, figures of speech, Rasa, import of the composition, the word, the sentence, grammatical categories like case, verb, gender, etc. and the work as a whole. Two other determinants are added in verse 40. These are prosodic features and sound effects. The author finally says that his list of determinants should be taken as illustrative rather than as exhaustive.

Kshemendra defines Auchitya as follows:

*Yatkila Yasyamanurupam taduchitmuchyate,*

*Yasya bhavamauchityam Kathayanti, i.e.*, a thing which suits another thing is called *proper* and the relation between what suits what is called *propriety* (prose commentary following verse 7).

*Auchityavicharcharcha* contains 40 theoretical statements in verse. Besides, these versified theorizings are interspersed with numerous citations from other works and writers and the author's own prose commentaries. The main purpose of this treatise seems to be to establish Auchitya as the central theory of poetics. Verse 3, for example, contains the author's testament of faith:

*Auchityasya chamatkarakarinashacharocharvane,*
*Rasajivitatabhutasya vicharamkuruteadhuna.*

I am now describing Auchitya which produces miracles in poetry and which is the soul of Rasa which, in turn, is the soul of poetry".

Verse 5 says:

*Alankarastvalankara guna eva gunah sada,*

*Auchitya rasasiddhasya sthiram kavyasyajivitam, i.e.,* Figures of speech and artistic devices decorate and beautify poetry but neither of them is its essence. The real essence of Rasa-saturated poetry is Auchitya".

Verse 6 adds:

*Uchitasthana vinyasadankritiralankriti,*

*Auchityadachyute nityambhavantyeva guna gunah, i.e.,* Figures of speech and poetic devices acquire their true and full meaning only when they adequately conform to the norms of propriety".

To sum up what has so far been said in this section, we may remind ourselves that creativity or literariness consists neither in a set of rules nor in flights of fancy alone; it consists in an imaginative coupling of freedom with restraint. The crux of the theory of Auchitya lies in reminding poets and critics alike that the practice of literature is a game which has a set of well-defined rules. As Rabindranath Tagore points out: "The beauty of the poem is bound by strict laws; yet it transcends them all. The laws are its wings; they do not keep it weighed down; they carry it to freedom. Its form is in law, but its spirit is in beauty. Law is the first step towards freedom and beauty is the complete liberation which stands and shines on the pedestal of law" (cited in Kuppuswami Shastri 1970).

## III

It may have become clear from the forgoing accounts of Auchitya and Decorum that the relationship between them does not require much interpretation. If we arrange these accounts side by side, the parallelism between the two theories will just shine out. The similarity between the two is not confined to an over-all conceptual dimension; it is also explicit and functional; it extends to the details. The theories and their developmental accounts are so close to each other that they impress us as alternative formulations of the same thing. We could, however, note the following features of the parallelism between Auchitya and Decorum:

Great proponents of the theory of literary propriety have shared views on its definition and scope. Bharata and Aristotle, Horace and Kshemendra, all agree on the essentiality of Auchitya/Decorum to the practice and criticism of literature. All of them agree that literary propriety has to be maintained with regard to action, situation, character and style. Aristotle requires the dramatist to differentiate between characters by sex, age, social class, profession and nationality (cf Hardison 1968: 202). Likewise, Bharata demands that in a play a character should be portrayed with due regard to his profession, skill, learning, family background, social status, etc.:

*Yadyasya karmam shilpaṃ va vidya va jatireva va,*
*Satena namna sambhasya natkadau prayoktibhih*

(NS, 19: 13)

Aristotle also requires the dramatist's presentation to take note of spectacle, of the actor's as well as the producer's arts (cf Hardison 1968: 215-16). Similarly, Bharata lays down that the dramatist must have an eye on costume-designing and make-up of characters (cf NS 23: 1-150). Aristotle insists on the aptness of speeches used by characters. He says: "Each class of men, each type of disposition, will have its own appropriate way of letting the truth appear .... [As] a rustic and educated man will not say the same things nor speak in the same way" and so differences of age, sex, nationality, profession, education, etc., have to be maintained in diction (cf *Rhetoric* 1408[a]). Bharata devotes large sections of chapters 18 and 19 of the *Natyashastra* (verses 31-55 & 1-12 respectively) to discuss speech varieties to be used by different types of characters in a play. Likewise, Horace argues that words must be appropriate to characters: "A lot depends on whether the speaker is a god or hero, a ripe old man or one who is still in the flush and flower of youth, a lady of high degree or a bustling nurse, a roaming merchant or one who tills a flourishing plot, a native of Thebes or Argos" (*Ars Poetica*).

Like the *Poetics* and the *Natyashastra*, the *Ars Poetica* and the *Auchityavicharcharcha* have several things in common. Both of these books are versified essays on literary propriety, both set up a comprehensive frame of reference for their central theory, both represent the final development of the theory and, finally, both establish propriety as an indispensable theory of literary criticism.

**Unique Similarities**

The two traditions of scholarship have similar views on the norms of propriety to which all works of art have to be subjected for a viable and responsible critical assessment and judgement. Horace, for example, proposes that the playwright worth his salt must "turn to life and behaviour for his dramatic models; the dramatist must know that what is required of a senator or of a judge cannot be required of a military general" (*Ars Poetica*). Similarly, Bharata and other Indian theorists suggest that in judging drama the ground of reference is the world. One has to know the infinite variety of human nature to achieve success in art (cf Raghavan). To quote Bharata: "*Tasmannatya prayogotu pramanam lokaishyate, i.e.*, the real touchstone of a play's success is conformity to the ways of the world" (NS, 26: 121). In the preceding verse of the same chapter Bharata observes that a play "does not realize its full meaning unless it depicts the reality of human nature and behaviour" (26: 120). Bhamah supports Bharata's dictum when he describes a play as "conforming to the ways of the world: *Yuktam lokasyabhavana*" (1: 21). Dandin puts it more emphatically: "Poetry which does not violate the truth of ordinary experience pleases all and is therefore the best poetry: *Kantam sarva jagatkantam laukikarthanatikramati*" (1: 85).

As regards the significance of the theory of propriety in literature, there is a very close similarity between Indian and Greek traditions. *Decorum*, says Milton, "is the grand masterpiece to observe", Kshemendra decrees that Auchitya is "the life-breath of poetry-*Auchityam Kavyasyajivitam*".

The striking similarity between the illustrations offered by the respective advocates of the two theories of what it is like when the rules of propriety are violated is really remarkable. At the beginning of the *Ars Poetica*, Horace remarks:

"Suppose a painter decided to set a human head
On a horse's neck, to lay various kinds of feather
On limbs which were such a jumble that the top
of a lovely woman
Ended up as the tail of a black and hideous fish-
And then asked you to see it, could you help laughing,
my friends?"

In the *Auchityavicharcharcha* Kshemendra wonders if "a woman wears a girdle round her neck, a necklace round her waist, anklets on her wrists, and bangles on her feet, who can restrain laughter at such a sight?

*Kanthe mekhalaya nitambhaphalake tarena harenava,*
*Panau nupurbandhanena charana keyurapashena va* (6).

Bharata also says: "*Mekhalorasi baddha tu hasyam samupapadyate*—a girdle worn at the breast produces only ridicule" (NS 23: 70). It is a violation of decorum, according to Bharata, for the dramatist to present a woman bemoaning separation from her lover as having her body decked with jewels (cf Raghavan 1970). Similarly, Goldsmith exclaims:

"What must be the entire perversion of scenical decorum, when, for instance, we see an actress ... unwieldy with fat endeavouring to convince the audience that she is dying with hunger" (*The Bee* Oct 6, 1759 cited in Gilbert 1970).

It has been noted above that a poet has to abide by the rules of poetry-writing in the same way that a squash-player has to conform to the rules of his game. Rules are necessary for every game, for every organized activity. They are also important. But we must be very clear about the relativity of rules and games. Rules are necessary and important, no doubt, but they do not make the game. No one can become a cricketer only by mastering the rules of cricket. Besides, there are different types of cricketers. They can easily be rated on the basis of their performance of the game. They are never rated with reference to their knowledge of the rules of the game. A player may know all the rules of the game and yet be part of the crowd. To stand above and apart from the crowd he needs much more. The knowledge of or conformity to technicality does not, and perhaps cannot, make a player or a poet a Bradman or an Eliot. Conformism is often a sign of mediocrity. It is no accident that great poets and players set their own standards, their own rules, as it were. It is the power of the man and the quality of his doing that sets a poet (or a player) above the crowd of poets (or players). The theory of literary propriety is concerned only with the technicality of doing literature and fortunately we have had remarkable poets and critics in both Indian and Greek traditions who could, at the right moment, remind their fellow poets and critics that a mechanical application of or adherence to the rules of propriety could lead to the production of a mere trash in the name of creative writing. Poetry is never done by the rule of thumb.

Abhinavagupta, the remarkable scholar-critic of the eleventh century, emphatically declares that the observance of Auchitya is a necessity in the practice of literature but it is only a means to an end. A critic, says Abhinavagupta, who regards Auchitya as an end in itself or as prior to other demands, is a critic who does not understand the *what* and the *why* of great poetry (cf Raghavan 1970). Similarly, Croce and Wordsworth have their serious reservations about following decorum to its logical end. Croce believes that poets are entitled to upset the rules of criticism because poetry is an art and all art is intuitive. Wordsworth, in his historic Preface to the *Lyrical Ballads* condemns the *poetic diction* and the *false refinement* of the Augustans (cf Herrick 1965).

There is, therefore, a broad consensus among writers on poetic decorum that in literature no law, convention or feature is an absolute; it all depends on 'how' and 'when' something is used in relation to something else. Since we can never be able to prepare a final inventory of what suits what in literature, every theory of decorum has to be flexible and open-ended. Any relation in literature, whether between the parts or between the parts and the whole or between one whole and another, which does not offend against the commonsense of the enlightened reader/listener/viewer is proper and fitting.

The sense of decorum lies not in the rigid prescription of absolute laws but in a tactful and flexible application of laws. Decorum is "very much alterable and subject to varietie", says Puttenham (cf Gilbert 1970 & Palmer 1973). Robert Bridges rightly lays down that in literature "no propriety is absurd if it is in Keeping" (1933). Similarly, Bhamah, Dandin and Rudrata decree that there are no absolute flaws and excellences in poetry and that everything depends on the context. We have already quoted Rudrata who says: "A word becomes awkward or rustic (*gramya*) when it does not fit in with the context: *Yadanuchitam yatra padam tattatraivapajayate gramyam*" (6: 17). A modern Western critic says exactly the same thing when he writes:

"Is any word artistically bad in itself?
Is not ain't an excellent expression
When placed in the mouth of an illiterate character in a play or story?"

(Spingarn cited in Raghavan 1970).

The crux of the theory of Auchitya decorum lies in an imaginative coupling of freedom and restraint, of convention and deviation, of the old and the new.

# 3

# The Freudian Paradigm of Literature

"It is the mark of an educated man to look for precision in each class of things just so far as the nature of the subject admits".

Aristotle—*Ethica Nicomachea* 1094b 25

♦

"There is nothing covered that shall not be revealed; and nothing hid that shall not be known".

*St Matthew* 10: 26

♦

"Humanity has always known it has a soul; it fell to me to show that it also has instincts".

Sigmund Freud cited in *Robert* 1966: 195

## I

### Freud: An Original Thinker of Modern Times

In his monumental biography of the master, Ernest Jones presents an immensely readable account of the various fascinating aspects of Freud's life and work. Freud was a voracious reader, an encyclopaedic scholar, an original thinker, a powerful writer, and an eloquent speaker. Freud was a polyglot; he knew languages like Latin, Greek, French, Italian, Spanish and English, besides Hebrew and German (Jones 1964: 49). Freud was a great lover; he wrote 900 letters to his betrothed, Martha Bernays, in the three years of separation from her between his engagement and marriage (p 109). He liked and enjoyed the company of intellectually 'masculine women', of whom there were several in his acquaintanceship, but, in his personal conduct, he always remained chaste, even to the point of being *puritanical*, and he consistently held that the destiny of women was determined by nature through beauty, charm and sweetness (pp 150, 238). Law and custom had yet to give women a lot but their position, Freud believed, must remain what it had been: "in youth an adored darling and in mature years a loved wife" (p 152).

Lionel Trilling (1964) in his excellent 'Introduction' to the abridged, one-volume edition of Jones' masterpiece, draws attention to Freud's amazing success in reconciling extremes in his life and character. Freud hated music and religious ceremonies but loved literature. He did not believe in God or in immortality—he was an unrepentant atheist—but he had full faith in the destiny of man. Freud knew that life was a grim, irrational and humiliating business but nothing could diminish his love of man. He had to undergo thirty-three harrowing operations for the cancer of the jaw in the last sixteen years of his life (i.e., 1923-39) but he could say: "I prefer to think in torment to not being able to think clearly". His capacity to think with clarity in torment is amply illustrated by his numerous books and lectures and by his uninterrupted professional engagements during those painful years. By the way, Freud's lack of faith in religion and God need not baffle or embarrass us; we need not deceive ourselves into thinking that *we* believe in religion and God. One of the most religious of men in history has it on record that there is no real difference between "the highest ecclesiastical giant who can talk by the volume and the lowest, most ignorant materialist .... we are all atheists; and yet we try to fight the man who admits it" (Vivekananda 1964: 172-73). Freud had, at least, the guts to announce his lack of faith in public. To continue with the paradoxical nature of his thinking, we must note that Freud always regarded the human condition with a wry irony but he fully enjoyed the fact of his having been born. He admired and respected many of his contemporaries, although he knew quite well that apparent respectability was not a conclusive evidence of people's inner goodness, rather, very often, it was the reverse. He took it as one of the highest aims of his life to expose hypocrisy and to explore the abysmal gap between appearance and reality in civilized conduct. Freud was, perhaps, the first psychologist who convincingly showed us that "most of what we are conscious of is not real and that most of what is real is not in our consciousness" (Fromm 1970: 14).

To many of his contemporaries Freud was a spell-binder and a hero whose life was an epic voyage of discovery. Within the first few weeks of his engagement, Freud wrote to Martha Bernays: "And when you are my dear wife before all the world and bear my name, we will pass our life in happiness for ourselves and earnest work for mankind until we have to close our eyes in eternal sleep and leave to those near us a memory everyone will be glad of" (Jones 1968: 138). Of his intellectual powers and scientific adventures, Freud was to write many years later: "I am not really a man of science, not an observer, not an experimenter, and not a thinker. I am nothing but by temperament a conquistador—an *adventurer*—if you want to translate the word, with the curiosity, the boldness, and the tenacity that belong to that type of being" (Trilling 1964). Freud's self-assessment is perhaps the best assessment of his life and work, of his mission and mode: he was an adventurer *par excellence*. Most people, even those hostile to his ideas, would perhaps agree that Freud undertook and completed his voyage of the unconscious with a sense of adventure.

There seems to be a broad concensus among critics about the historic role that Freud played in shaping and influencing modern thinking about the human mind. Like the theory of evolution or the cosmological doctrine of the planetary system, Freud's theory of the mind is "an integral part of modern thinking" (Cioffi 1973) and a tribute to "the power of consecutive thought" (Roazen 1973). Like Darwin and Copernicus, Freud can be regarded as "a moulder of thought rather than as a mere discoverer of facts" (Brown 1961: 2). Freud is one of "those few pioneers whose discoveries have altered the whole texture of our thinking about human behaviour" (Duke 1972:7), so much so, that even those "who most violently denounce his views attack them in Freudian cliches and arguments which would have been incomprehensible had he never existed" (Brown 1961:2). Freud led people to think about their thinking and feeling, self-knowledge and self-deceit, success and failure in ways that would have seemed to earlier generations "at once scandalous and silly. It would be hard to find in the history of ideas, even in the history of religion, someone whose influence was so immediate, so broad and so deep" (Wollheim 1971: 9). Thomas Mann compares Freud to Schopenhauer: "Freud is an artist of thought like Schopenhauer, and like him, a writer of European rank" (1973). Even critics like D H Lawrence, Carl Jung and Eric Fromm, acknowledge Freud's great influence on twentieth century thinking about man. As early in 1923, Lawrence wrote that the *Oedipus Complex* had become "a household word, a commonplace of tea-table chat" (cited in Cioffi 1973). According to Jung, it was only an idealist like Freud who could devote "a life-time to the unclean work" of digging up the unconscious (1963). It was only Freud, says Jung elsewhere, who liberated us from the "unhealthy pressure of an ancient world of rotten habits" and showed us what a "sentimental•fraud" it was on the part of parents to claim that "they live only for their children", or that of the noble son who "is at his mother's feet all his life" or that of the ideal daughter who has "a perfect understanding of her father" (1973). Fromm is of the view that Freud "did for psychology what great dramatists and novelists had achieved in artistic form. He showed man as the hero of a drama who, even if he is only of average talent, is a hero because he fights passionately in the attempt to make some sense of the fact of having been born" (1970: 50).

The most important contribution of Freud seems to be in the realm of thinking about the unconscious motivations of human behaviour. Whether we agree with him or not is not important; what really matters is the fact that he has changed our world view. Most critics will accept Cioffi's observation as a statement of fact: "we shall never again be where we were; that though the extent, and even the precise character of Freud's scientific achievement will remain a matter of dispute for some time to come, what is not disputable is that Freud broke down, and not just momentarily, one of the solitudes in which we lived" (1973). Interestingly enough, Freud was himself aware of this part of his contribution: "I belonged to those who, according to Hebbel's expression, "have disturbed the world's sleep" (1938: 943). Referring to Freud's historic lecture tour of America in 1909 his biographer records: "From now on he might meet with misunderstanding, criticism, opposition, and even abuse, but he could no longer be ignored" (Jones 1964: 349). If a thinker cannot be ignored, he must be great, whatever may be the typology of his greatness.

In spite of his own statement that he was not a scientist, Freud believed that his 'creation', *psychoanalysis*, was a science and that it must be so considered (cf Freud 1938: 933, Brown 1961: 1, Blum 1969: 2, McGlashan & Reeve 1970: 7). Freud himself says: "I treated my discoveries as ordinary contributions to science and hoped that they would be received in the same spirit" (cited in Robert 1966: 151). Now, the question is: What is science? Or, What distinguishes a scientific enquiry from a non-scientific enquiry? There is really no need here to volunteer a definition of science. There is already a universal and time-honoured consensus about what is science or scientific. However, there is some need for people outside the sciences "proper" to realize that the label "science" or "scientific" cannot and must not be used for anything and everything under the sun, for, the craze to use such terms in a loose sense can easily convert science into *scientism*, and sometimes, even into *occultism.* To make the distinction clear, let us take an example. Numerologists, all the world over, tend to believe that numerology is a "science". Numerology, as we all know, is the study of numbers, and it assigns to numbers certain properties and attributes. In numerology, all primary numbers, i.e., 1 to 9, are believed to have certain easily identifiable properties. The number 9, for example, is regarded as a symbol of Mars, the god of War, and, as such, represents determination, heroism and independence of mind (cf Shreemali 1984: 129-131). Let us take a specific instance. Suppose we want the numerologist to tell us something general about all those years in the calendar which have 9 as the terminal figure. The numerologist might formulate some such generalizations as the following:

(i) Years ending in 9 witnessed great revolutions—revolutions which gave new directions to human history, (ii) such years produced men who turned out to be extraordinary leaders in various fields, viz., religion, politics, science, literature, etc. (iii) such years were years of most unfortunate deaths or executions. Beginning with the last, the numerologist might offer concrete illustrations. Some of the most regrettable deaths or executions which occurred in such years were: Socrates (399 BC), Jesus Christ (AD 29), George Washington (1779) and Humboldt (1859). As for the second generalization, a number of great names could be mentioned: Lord Mahavira (599 BC), Socrates (469 BC), Prophet Mohammed (AD 569?), Machiavelli (1469), Guru Nanak (1469), Racine (1639), Johnson (1709), Napoleon (1769), Darwin (1809), Lincoln (1809), Gandhi (1869), Stalin (1879), Einstein (1879), Nehru (1889), and Martin Luther King (1929). Similarly, to illustrate the first generalization, the numerologist can easily refer to such events as: Francis of Assissi issued the first rules of his brotherhood in 1209, Joan of Arc raised the siege of Orleans in 1429, Queen Elizabeth I succeeded to the throne in 1559, the Divine Right of Kings in England was abolished in 1689, the French Revolution began and George Washington was elected the first president of America in 1789, the Treaty of Versailles was signed in 1919, the Indian National Congress adopted the resolution for complete independence for the first time in 1929, World War II began in 1939 and the first Socialist Government in China began in 1949 (for details cf Grun 1975: 96-463). Besides, Darwin published *The Origin of Species* and Marx published his first book on political philosophy in 1859. Freud had three crucial 9s in his life: publication of *The Interpretation of Dreams* in 1899, American tour in 1909 and death in 1939. The publication year of *The Interpretation of Dreams* did not only combine the three 9s in Freud's life but also made it the third constituent of the trilogy which exerted so much influence on later history. Marx, Darwin and Freud are names which have never been ignored. 1899 is also reducible to 9 by the simple process of left-to-right addition. Number 9, the numerologist would further tell us, is the highest primary number and it is the only number which, multiplied by any number, reproduces itself by the same process of left-to-right addition. On the basis of all these facts the numerologists draws the final and specious conclusion : "If a year in the calendar has 9 as its terminal figure, then it must be a turning-point in human history".

At this point, certain questions suggest themselves: What does this conclusion prove? How valid are the generalizations on which it is based? How adequate is its statistics? Is there a logical connection between the year which has 9 as its terminal figure and the especial events of that year? If one starts counting the years ending in 9 from 600 BC, one can point to a total of 258 such years in the calendar upto 1986, while examples cited by the numerologist come to only 27. The numerologist's hypothesis is thus based on very poor statistics. It covers only about 10.4 per cent of the total number of years in which 9 happens to be the last figure. Similarly, in Freud's life there were nine 9s out of which only 33 per cent are covered by the numerologist's statistics. A hypothesis which is built on such inadequate data cannot be a scientific hypothesis. Numerology is a variant of occultism, not that of science and, if anyone uses the term *science* to refer to it, such usage must be considered metaphoric or laymanish.

**Paradigm: A well-defined Pattern**

Every scientific enquiry is carried on within a given *paradigm.* A paradigm is, roughly speaking, a set of shared assumptions about the nature of the phenomena, the nature of relevant questions to be asked about the phenomena, the nature of the technique to be used in seeking solutions and the goal or goals to be achieved. One of the basic requirements of a paradigm is to ensure that it has identified the right problem, asked the right questions, used the right technique and that its facts are generalizable. Further, it is obligatory for a paradigm to ensure that the problem is significant, the data is adequate, the relation of the facts to the theory is legitimate and that it is able to *explain* all observed phenomena and to *predict* phenomena yet unobserved. A paradigm is a well-defined, consistent, explicit and goal-oriented model or pattern. Generalizations within a paradigm must be objectively verifiable or, to use Karl Popper's term, *testable* (Magee 1973: 26). Generalizations in science must be so designed as can be easily proved or falsified, confirmed or refuted, because scientific knowledge is "of its nature provisional" (p 26). Succeeding theories in science do only confirm "the permanently conjectural nature of scientific knowledge" (p 28). The scientist, *qua* scientist, is aware that every theory is replaceable by a better theory because his real concern in the pursuit of knowledge is to get closer and closer to the truth. It is, therefore, obligatory for the scientist who seeks to bring about a revolution in his field of activity to formulate a paradigm which is sufficiently unprecedented and sufficiently open-ended because a *scientific revolution* begins with the transition from an old to a new paradigm (cf Kuhn 1970: 90). A change of paradigm entails a change of attitude to the universe, or, at least, to the relevant phenomena. The transfer of allegiance from paradigm to paradigm is a *conversion experience* for the scientific community (p 151) and all conversions, whether religious or secular, are resisted by people who have well-defined loyalties to the existing paradigm. It is to persuade such unwilling scientific communities that the revolutionary scientist has to fulfill the basic requirements mentioned above. The history of science is the history of cycles of revolution and changes of paradigm.

This study is intended to examine (i) Freud's general paradigm of psychic life and (ii) his specific paradigm of literature on the assumption that the complex of Freud's premises, techniques, goals and solutions constitute a framework which can be designated as a paradigm in psychology. A paradigm in a social science like psychology is not normally expected to be of the same level of sophistication as its counterpart in physics or mathematics because the nature of the subject does not admit that degree of precision which generally goes with the physical sciences. A paradigm in psychology is ultimately a watered-down version of a strictly scientific paradigm. But, since psychology (psychoanalysis, to be more correct) has a claim to science, its paradigms must be judged by criteria which distinguish science from mere *scientism* or sheer *occultism*. Freud dealt with a significant problem, asked questions which he thought were relevant to his method of enquiry, used a well-defined technique and set up a specific goal. The problem was psychic life, the questions and technique were related to free association and psychoanalysis and the goal to be achieved was an adequate structural description of the mind. Freud's laudable aim was defined in his motto: "The Ego shall be where the Id was".

Academic psychology before Freud had been content to observe and describe mental phenomena; Freud saw the need to *explain* it (cf Brown 1961: 2). It was not an easy task. The human psyche may not be a very profitable field for investigation. An investigation into the life of the mind may be overflooded with wild conjectures and the investigator may lose sight of his track and final goal. *Psychoanalysis*, said Freud, had "never claimed to give a perfect theory of the human psychic life" (1938: 965). Psychoanalysis may not have given a *perfect* theory, but it has certainly given a theory of mind. It has a set of premises, a neatly defined area of investigation and an elaborate technical vocabulary and with all these, seeks to offer a set of generalizations about various aspects of psychic life: its structure, function, nature, motivations, mechanisms and aims. All these components constitute a paradigm which is *testable* in the sense of being able to be confirmed or falsified. Does Freud's paradigm explain *all* the facts of psychic life? Can it *predict* the psychic behaviour of humans yet unborn? Are its generalizations objectively verifiable? Are its major premises sound and its conclusions valid? Is psychoanalysis a science? Can a work of art or the psychic life of a poet be amenable to a scientific investigation? An attempt will be made in the following pages to answer these questions.

Before we proceed further, it will be useful to make a few clarifications. The first clarification concerns the distinction between 'instinct' and 'drive'. An instinct, for Freud, is an inherited, unchangeable and automatic response to specific stimuli. A drive, on the other hand, is a response which is capable of infinite variations through experience. Freud's term for *drive* was *Trieb* in German, the plural being *Triebe* (cf Brown 1961: 10 & Blum 1969: 3-4). Freud did not use the German 'Instinkt' (which is *instinct* in English). However, in English translations of the psychoanalytic literature terms like *instinct*, *drive* and *impulse* are used interchangeably and so are they used in this study. Secondly, although in Freudian literature *sex* and *sexuality* are used as synonyms, a sharp distinction is drawn in this study between these terms. The third clarification concerns the separation between Freud's general paradigm of psychic life and his specific paradigm of literature drawn in this study, although there is no such distinction in Freud's writings. His views on literature are an integral part of his views on psychic life. The distinction drawn here should, therefore, be taken in the sense of just a mental abstraction. The use of the term *paradigm* is made here only to invite attention to the urgency of examining Freud's views on literature, as well as on psychic life, from the scientific point of view. It is one of the subsidiary aims of this study to show that in the vast corpus of Freud's writings the amount of literary criticism is very little because Freud was never interested in the study of literature as an independent pursuit. Those who would be looking for more literature than psychoanalysis in this chapter will, therefore, be disappointed. This chapter is an attempt to examine Freud's understanding and analysis of literature and not an attempt to impose literature on Freud. Those who appreciate this constraint will be forgiving.

## II

Ernest Jones in his biography of Freud suggests that the most profitable way of evaluating Freudianism or psychoanalysis (the two terms are synonymous) is to set it in the historical perspective and to study it as "an historical evolution, never as the perfected body of knowledge" (1964: 26). A reader of Jones' book can readily gather support for this point of view from what T S Eliot once wrote on the poet's relation to his tradition: "No poet, no artist of any art has his complete meaning alone. His significance, his appreciation is the appreciation of his relation to the dead poets and artists. You cannot value him alone, you must set him for contrast and comparison, among the dead" (1953). Since sex or sexuality (i.e., another set of synonyms in Freudian literature), both adult and infantile (perhaps more infantile than adult), is the nucleus of the Freudian paradigm, it is necessary to take a brief survey of the scattered views on the subject, treating such a jumble of views as the pre-paradigm stage in the evolution of the theory of sex, before we discuss Freud's paradigm. It would be interesting to see these views against the backdrop of Henry James' remark that "sex is something about which we think a great deal when we are not thinking about anything else" (quoted in Burke 1973: 264). Do we think about sex only in the hours of idleness as James would have us believe? The following paragraphs will, among other things, provide an answer to this question.

**Sex: A Dominant Constituent of Human Thinking**

Sex has always been considered one of the most dominant urges of human thinking and behaviour. Anatole France, the great French poet, at the age of 60, talking to his private secretary and mistress, M Brouson, confided: "There is only one science—lamour—carnal love; all else is vanity" (quoted in Das 1949: 75). Isadora Duncan, the distinguished Wagnerian opera dancer, records in her autobiography her confrontations with Gabrielle D Annunzio, the famous Italian poet, dramatist, novelist and war hero, in these words: "He said to me: Every night I am coming to your room (in a hotel) at two o'clock. I have conquered all women in the world, but I have yet to conquer Isadora" (Das 1949: 79). Commenting on Wagner and his opera, Isadora writes: "The closed grotto of satyrs and nymphs and Venus was the closed grotto of Wagner's mind, exasperated by continual longing for sensual outlet which he finds only within his own imagination" (Das p 82). An ancient Sanskrit text advocates that it is "permissible to satisfy carnal desires in dreams: *Svapneshu agamayaa-gamanam prashastam*" (Das, p 124). This ancient Sanskrit text reminds one of what Plato once wrote about the so-called virtuous man: "The virtuous man contents himself with dreaming that which the wicked man does in actual life" (Jastrow 1949: 34-35). Nietzsche's sweeping generalization about the ubiquity of the sexual impulse is rather frighteningly instructive: "The degree and essential nature of any human being's sexuality extends into the highest pinnacle of his spirit" (cited in Greer 1973: 67).

The pre-paradigm period of the theory of sex is full of references to what Freud designated as *infantile sexuality*. The infant in Blake's poem ('Infant Sorrow') does not find solace anywhere except on the mother's breast :

"Bound and weary I thought best
To sulk upon my mothers breast" (Greer p 71).

That the infant is a veritable Oedipus is amply illustrated by what Stendhal says in *Henri Brulard* about his infantile experiences with his mother: "I wanted to cover my mother with kisses, and for her to have no clothes on. She loved me passionately and kissed me often. I returned her kisses with such ardor that she was sometimes obliged to run away. I abhorred my father when he came to interrupt our kisses. I always wanted to kiss her bosom" (cited in Hall 1963: 157). There is a similar perception of infant sexuality in Diderot's *Rameau's Nephew* (1762): "If the little savage (i.e., the child) were left to himself, if he preserved all his foolishness and combined the violent passions of a man of thirty with the lack of reason of a child in the cradle, he'd wring his father's neck and go to bed with his mother" (cited in Trilling 1972).

Before the present discussion proceeds any further, it is necessary to be clear about the two distinctive features of the pre-paradigm conception of sex. These features are not explicitly mentioned in any of the conceptions which, for us, constitute the pre-paradigm stage of the theory of sex; they have to be deduced from stray remarks such as those quoted above and those to be quoted below. In the first place, it should be noted that every organism, as an organism, has two innately specified, basic urges: the urge for the survival and preservation of the organism itself and the urge for the survival and preservation of the species to which the organism belongs. The organism has to satisfy the urge for hunger so that it survives and continues to be and it has to fulfil the urge for sex so that the species survives and continues to be. The purpose of eating is self-preservation and the purpose of sex is species-preservation. The two types of preservation are interdependent; the one cannot exist without the other. Secondly, these two preservations are obligatory for each organism and its species. Neither the species nor the organism can choose to dispense with either sort of preservation and, since there is no choice, there is no morality involved here. The two preservative urges, i.e., the self-preservative and species-preservative (hunger and sex) are therefore amoral. In other words, they are above and beyond morality. Thirdly, these urges are *organism-uniform* and *organism-specific*, i.e., *all* organisms have these urges and that *only* organisms have these urges. As these innate, basic urges are shared by *all* organisms and *only* by organisms, we cannot have a scale of values to distinguish one organism from another organism. No organism is better or worse than any other organism in so far as hunger and sex are concerned. Man is at one with the lowest forms of life in respect of hunger and sex. There is absolutely no distinction between the highest and the lowest in the twin realms of survival and preservation. All created beings are equal here.

**Nature of Sex**

The second clarification concerns the nature of sex. When we talk about the nature of sex with reference to the pre-Freudian stage of its theory, we must distinguish between two forms of sex: the one that is genetically transmitted and the other that is culturally transmitted. For want of a better set of terms we might designate the genetic form as *sex* and its cultural variant as *sexuality.* As non-humans do not have *culture* (at least in our sense of the term), they have only sex. Darwin believed that in the process of evolution man acquired reasoning ability and that this reasoning ability, in course of time, became his "special form of adaptation, a compensation for his weakness and a means of attaining his physiological needs" (McGlashan & Reeve 1970: 15). Darwin further pointed out that a human being is fundamentally an animal, "propelled by animal passions and instincts, who, by evolution, has managed to attain a veneer of intellectual control which animals do not possess" (p 15). Sexuality is thus a gift of human evolution. Now, man has both, innate sex and acquired sexuality. To put it differently, while sex is common to all organisms including man, sexuality is peculiar to the *homo sapiens* alone. Sexuality is the special privilege of the *homo sexualis*—the modern, social, political, conscientious, religious, rational, cultured and wise man. Sex is necessary and benign because it is structurally pure and motivationally innocent, even pious, while sexuality is superfluous and malignant because it is structurally a hybrid of a physiological impulse and reasoning power and by nature volatile, chameleon-like, satanic and highly motivated. Sex is always heterosexual. It is always a matter of physical union between two adults of different sexes in which the female takes the initiative and the male only cooperates. Sex is an urge or an act which is performed with the specific aim of reproduction, i.e., the preservation of the species. It is therefore always open. Sexuality, on the other hand, can be either hetero or homosexual, even autosexual. It has nothing to do with reproduction. Reproduction for sexuality is an accident rather than a design. It is not limited to adulthood; it is coterminous with life, from the cradle to the grave, because it is not a basic, physiological impulse; it becomes amorphous, surreptitious, aggressive and masculine. In respect of sexuality the woman is generally a dupe, an unwilling partner or a helpless victim. But the most pernicious aspect of sexuality is its basic psychic determination. Sexuality is basically and, more importantly, a psychic demand and a psychic act and, therefore, it is more harmful to the life of the spirit. Physical sexuality is a mere momentary aberration while psychic sexuality is a perpetual degeneration, all-pervasive and all-consuming. As physical sexuality is only a superficial manifestation of the psychic, it is psychic sexuality and pollution that is condemned by those who look upon the true expansion of the spirit as the highest peak of human development. Look at the following verse in the Gospel: "Ye have heard that it was said by them of old time, Thou shalt not commit adultery: But I say unto you, That whosoever looketh on a woman to lust after her hath committed adultery with her already in his heart" (St Matthew 5: 27-8). The medieval Hindi saint-poet Kabeer (1398-1518) would have said: "Think of the fruit on the tree and you've destroyed its virginity". A man becomes what he thinks. The thinking man is the real man while the doing man is just a passing phase. Whether a man is correct or corrupt depends upon what he does within his psyche: "There is nothing from without a man, that entering into him can defile him: but the things which come out of him, those are they that defile the man" (St Mark 7: 15).

In view of the distinction drawn above between the two forms of sex, one can safely generalize that sex is the law of life as it enables the organism to fulfil and flourish, while sexuality is the negation of life, as it is unnecessary, anarchic and destructive. This sort of distinction between sex and sexuality can be supported from certain verses in the *Manusmriti* and the *Geeta*. The *Manusmriti* says:

*"Na mansa bhakshane dosho,*
*Na madye, na cha maithune,*
*Pravritiresha bhutanam*
*Nivritirastu mahaphala*, i.e.,

There is no sin in eating meat, in drinking spirituous liquor and in sexual act, for that is the natural way of created beings; but abstention (from these) brings great rewards" (cf Muller 1964: 177).

The *Manusmriti* goes on to say that sex for procreation is the law of life (i.e., *Dharma*) but sex for a purpose other than procreation is sexuality (i.e., *Kama*). Manu describes the first child born out of wedlock as *Dharmaja* (born out of a sense of Dharma or the law of life) and subsequent children as *Kamaja* (born out of *kama* or sexuality). The concept of marriage as a sacrament is a further confirmation of the indispensability of sex in the life of the individual. In a chapter devoted to the discussion of the duties of a householder, Manu prescribes three obligations that a householder has, respectively, to the gods, the ancestors and the seers (*Devarina, Pitririna* and *Rishirina*) and says that one who seeks final liberation without having studied the Vedas, without having begotten sons and without having offered sacrifices, sinks downward (cf 6: 35,36 & 37). In these verses sex is clearly linked with procreation which is the culmination of conjugal cooperation.

Our distinction between sex and sexuality seems to be implicit in the following verse of the *Bhagavadgeeta* :

*"Balam balavatam chaham*
*kamaraga vivarjitam'*
*Dharma viruddho bhuteshu*
*Kamosmi Bharatarshabha,* i.e.,

I am the strength of the strong, above sexuality and attachment. But, in created beings, I am sex which is not contrary to law, O Lord of Bharata" (9: 11).

The words of the Lord clearly means that sex is the law of life while sexuality is contrary to this law. The two occurrences of kama must be translated differently because they obviously mean two different things. The Lord is, at a time, kama and beyond kama. The parallel between this verse and the verse from the *Manusmriti* quoted above (5:56) is amazing: in both these verses, sex is said to be common to all organisms and, as such, it is in consonance with the law of life. The translation of the other form of kama as 'sexuality' is also supported by the psychogenetic description of this impulse in chapter II verses 62, 67, 70 and 71 in the *Geeta* and by the contrast made between Dharmaja and Kamaja in the *Manusmriti*. According to the psychogenesis of sexuality given in the *Geeta*, any centrifugal, object-oriented movement of the mind produces an effect in psychic life which ultimately becomes an impulse of sexuality. Verse 62 in chapter II, for example, makes it absolutely clear:

*"Dhyayato vishayan punsah*
*sangasteshupajayate;*
*Sangat sanjayato kamah*
*kamat krodhobhijayate,* i.e.,

When a man's mind is directed towards the objects of sense, attachment to them is produced. From attachment arises sexuality and from (the nonfulfilment of) sexuality results anger (and frustration)".

Once a separation between sex and sexuality is made, it becomes easy to see how and why sexuality transgresses all limits and takes multitudinous forms. Once sex ceases to be just a natural urge and a purely somatic function, it enters into the world of the psyche and sexualizes the entire mechanics of thinking. When sex is coupled with thinking, it becomes sexuality, which is capable of taking an infinite variety of forms and of drawing satisfaction in innumerable ways. As Don Juan tells Ana in Shaw's play:

"Do you not know that where there is a will there is a way? That whatever man really wishes to do he will finally discover a means of doing" (Shaw 1946: 158).

Freud hypothesized that sexuality was a *conscious* and *motivated* psychic function and that it was uniformly operative in *all* human beings, including the good and the great. This was certainly too radical, shocking and frightening a hypothesis to be accepted by the self-righteous. There were loud protests and vehement denials from all concerned. The next section is a brief chronicle of Freud's hypothesis and its repercussions.

III

**Theory of Mind**

Freud presents a model of the mind in one of his earliest and least known books: *The Project for a Scientific Psychology* (1895). The model (cf Wollheim 1971: 42-64) posits two structural components of the mind and its principle of operation. The mental apparatus is constructed out of two 'units of structure' or `material particles' known as *neurones*. The mind is structurally a complex network of sensory neurones which receive energy from stimuli and motor neurones which control the discharge of energy. The working principle of the mental apparatus is governed by the general laws of motion. The flow of energy or quantity, known as Q, through the network of neurones (sensory and motor) operates in accordance with the principle of *neuronic inertia* or the `constancy principle'. According to the constancy principle, the apparatus has a tendency to divest itself of energy or to reduce tension where tension is identified with the accumulation of energy and relief with its expulsion. Freud postulates two functions, primary and secondary, to explain the movement of energy in and out of the mind. According to the 'primary function' of the constancy principle, the mind seeks to reduce tension to zero, in other words, to expel all energy as and when it enters the system. However, the flow of energy is complicated by a particular psychic phenomenon. The mind receives energy not only from external stimuli but also from the inside, from the cells of the body. The energy that arises from such endogenous stimuli and corresponds to the major human needs of hunger, respiration and sex cannot be discharged immediately and totally. Such energy arising from internal stimuli cannot be discharged until suitable conditions are available in the external world. Now, if the environment does not cooperate with the mind in discharging tension, the mental apparatus must learn to engage in 'specific actions'. These specific actions enable the psychic apparatus to free itself from its continuous dependence on the environment, to tolerate accumulated energy till appropriate conditions are available. The mind still works according to the constancy principle but this principle now so functions as to credit the mind with the aim not of altogether eliminating tension but of keeping it as low as possible. The psychic function, so modified, is called the 'secondary function'. According to the *Project*, the sources of disturbance within the psychic apparatus lie in the inherent inadequacy of the primary function or in the failure of the mind to successfully engage itself in the secondary function. In other words, the life of the mind becomes vulnerable, particularly because it has to cope with the duality of the primary and the secondary functions. The mind has a natural tendency to reduce tension either totally and immediately or partly and slowly, but even that is not possible sometimes. In situations when the environment does not allow even partial release of tension, the mind is threatened by a critical law-and-order problem, as it were. Such situations make the psychic world a highly explosive zone for the suffering individual.

The theory of the mind, as summarized above, provides a general outline of the Freudian paradigm. All the important tenets of his study of the mind derive from and refer to the skeleton outlined in the *Project*. Freud wrote a number of books in the years to follow but the *Project* remained, till the end of his career, his major theoretical statement. A necessary corollary of this theoretical statement is Freud's adherence to a system of enquiry which sees the mind in terms of a duality. Freud once said of himself: "An intimate friend and a hated enemy have always been indispensable to my emotional life" (Duke 1972: 28) and this provides a clue to his life-long commitment to the analysis of the human psyche in terms of a duality. Man is both flesh and spirit, reason and emotion, saint and sinner, and the whole system of dynamic forces (i.e., the psyche) springs from the tension between these two opposites (cf Storr 1973: 80). Helmholtz (a famous determinist of the nineteenth century) thought of the world as being composed of a dynamic system of forces and believed that all physical energy could be reduced to *attraction and repulsion* (McGlashan & Reeve 1970: 14). Charles Darwin thought of the human mind as an evolving system, as a process of continual change, in which the biological and the intellectual forces wrestle with each other (p 15). Like Helmholtz and Darwin, Freud believes in the dual nature of man and proposes that man at his best, as man at his worst, is subject to a common set of explanations: that "all good and evil grow from a common process" (Bruner 1973: 140). Freud sees the human mind as an interplay of opposite tendencies or forces: tension and release, sex and hunger, love and hate, life and death. Whether he views love, the unconscious or sexuality, Freud sees an ambivalence, an opposition, everywhere. He does not find any human tendency which is pure and simple. Every human tendency, like every part of the human personality, contains an internal opposition. The unconscious contains elements from both "the highest and the lowest in man" (Jones 1964: 244) and, similarly, sexuality contains within itself the highest and the lowest in man: "from heaven through the world to hell" (Freud 1938: 572). Freud always maintains a distinction between two types of drives within the psyche. The theory of repression depends on his perception of such a duality of drives, if not "to provide the motive for repression, then, at any rate, to account for its mechanism. Remove the duality, and the whole theory of psychoneurosis would surely crumble" (Wollheim 1971: 179). Freud's theory of psychoneurosis, as of any other psychic phenomenon, rests on a duality of drives. Whether we talk of his early opposition between the sexual and the self-preservative drives, his middle period distinction between sexuality and ego-instincts or of his final duality of Eros and Thanatos, we always discover his insistence on viewing the human psyche, and, by extension, human society and human history, as the arenas for the warring impulses of love and hate, attraction and repulsion, life and death (cf Brown 1961: 27, Wollheim 1971: 179 & Fromm 1970: 50). According to the fully developed hypothesis, there are two basic instincts; a life instinct or Eros and a death instinct or Thanatos. The life instinct comprises the old concept of libido and part of the self-preservative drive. The death instinct is a force which is constantly working towards extinction and a return to the original inorganic state of complete freedom from tension. The death instinct contains a 'repetition compulsion' to return to an earlier state where there was no tension. Eros has the tendency to unite and to integrate; Thanatos has the opposite tendency to disintegration and destruction, even self-destruction. Both these drives operate constantly within man, fight each other, and blend with each other, until Thanatos proves to be stronger and has its ultimate triumph in the death of the individual. Writing in the final period of his career, Freud observes: "Our views have from the first been *dualistic* and today they are even more definitely dualistic than before - now that we describe the opposition as being, not between ego-instincts and sexual instincts but between life instincts and death instincts" (cited in Wollheim 1971: 180). George Santyana congratulates Freud for describing the mind in terms of a duality: "I am glad that Freud has resisted the tendency to represent [the] principle of love as the only principle in nature. Unity somehow exercises an evil spell over metaphysics .... I think pure unity is no less barren and graceless in metaphysics. You must have plurality to start with, or trinity, or at least duality, if you wish to get anywhere .... Freud, like Empedocles, has prudently introduced a prior principle for love to play with.... the tendency towards peace and death" (1973).

After a brief discussion of Freud's theory and methodology, as presented in the foregoing paragraphs, we can now turn to a relatively detailed consideration of the central tenets of Freudianism. The three basic postulates of the general Freudian paradigm are:

(i) that most of the individual's psychic processes are *unconscious;*

(ii) that all human behaviour is *motivated* and *goal-directed,* the motivating force being sexuality and the goal being the optimal satisfaction of the sexual drive;

(iii) and that, since the undisguised and instantaneous satisfaction of the sexual drive is incompatible with civilised behaviour, such drives have to be *repressed* or deliberately shifted from the conscious to the unconscious region of the human psyche (cf Brown 1961: 1- 35, Riviere 1973 & Guerin *et al* 1979: 123-131).

**Theory of the Unconscious**

Freud was indeed a revolutionary thinker but it would be preposterous to assume that whatever Freud did was original. The unconscious, for example, was not a Freudian discovery; both the term and the concept had been used by a variety of poets, philosophers and thinkers like Liebnitz, Schopenhauer, Bergson and Hartmann (cf Riviere 1973 & Brown 1961: 18). Freud, of course, discovered a descriptive framework for the unconscious. Disclaiming the title of the 'discoverer' of the unconscious on his seventieth birthday, Freud remarked: "The poets and philosophers before me discovered the unconscious; what I discovered was the *scientific method* by which the unconscious can be studied" (cited in Trilling 1970: 47). Freud's originality in the study of the unconscious has been identified in three respects: (i) he founded a theory of the mind or the 'science of the irrational', (ii) he offered a structural description of the mind in terms of three types of psychic processes and three psychic zones and (iii) he recognized the unconscious as a powerful domain or kingdom which determines all psychic behaviour (cf Brown 1961: 18-19). Freud's theory of the unconscious is acclaimed as "one of the most decisive steps in our knowledge of man and in our capacity to distinguish appearance from reality in human behaviour" (Fromm 1970: 15). It was this theory which sought to explain the why's of human behaviour by demonstrating a causal link between such concrete and observable phenomena as dreams, neuroses, perversions, sleeps, jokes and works of art, on the one hand, and the determination of such phenomena in the deepest substratum of the unconscious on the other. In Freud's diagrammatic representation of the unconscious, preconscious and conscious processes and of the triad of psychic zones—the id, the ego and the superego—the deepest and largest part of the psychic territory is shown as occupied by the unconscious. The conscious occupies only the tip of the territory while the preconscious is the no-man's land between the appeasing conscious and the demanding unconscious. The id is entirely unconscious while only a small portion of each of the ego and the superego is conscious. A chaos or cauldron of seething excitations, devoid of any internal organization or purposefulness, characterized by a tremendous and amorphous vitality, completely oblivious of any moral good or evil and blatantly supercilious to social values, the rambunctious *id* functions only in accordance with the *pleasure principle* to obtain optimal gratification of libidonous drives, ever remaining unmindful of the hazardous consequences its crazy pursuits might lead it to. Those who are sceptical of Freud's picture of the id may be reminded of St Paul's words: "the good that I would I do not, and that which I hate I do" (cf Duke 1972: 8-9) or of the Devil's proclamation in *Man and Superman*:

"From the beginning of my career I knew I should win in the long run by sheer weight of public opinion, in spite of the long campaign of misrepresentation and calumny against me. At bottom the universe is a constitutional one; and with such a majority as mine I cannot be kept permanently out of office" (Shaw 1946: 139).

As regulating agencies of the mind, the ego and the superego, acting in accordance with the *reality principle* and the *morality principle,* respectively, can, at best, form an alliance with the id so that both the individual and the society survive in an atmosphere of give-and-take, if not, in the ideal one of peaceful co-existence. The alliance of the id, the ego and the superego must, at best, be considered a league of equals; it can never be a military hierarchy in which the vigilant superior has a right to upbraid the erring subordinate by using, if necessary, the threat of a possible courtmartial. The psychic alliance, at its best, again, seeks to achieve a series of *compromise solutions* so that things go all right. If the alliance fails to collaborate or cohere, the consequence is perversion or neurosis.

The second major premise of Freud concerns the motivation of human behaviour and is based on the law of psychic causality or determinism. Everything that man does, Freud believes, must be an answer to a 'why', whether overt or covert. Throughout his career, Freud felt sure of the universal validity of the assumption that each individual, whether normal or neurotic, manifests a logical continuity in his psychic life and that each bit of human behaviour, whether a joke, or slip, a dream or a work of art, is motivated (cf Richards 1976 & Brown 1961: 3-4). Not only that, Freud consistently held that each bit of human behaviour is ultimately motivated by sexuality.

**Freud's Views on Sex-Sexuality**

It has already been pointed out in section I that in Freudian literature 'sex' and 'sexuality' are used interchangeably. What needs to be added here is that, irrespective of whether he uses sex or sexuality, Freud always talks about sexuality, as the term has been defined in section II. Here, a word of caution is necessary. In the previous section sexuality was held to be destructive and undesirable, while in Freud's scheme one specific form of sexuality (i.e., genital sexuality) is held to be necessary and, hence, desirable, although even that form of sexuality is carefully separated from the instinct for *procreation* (cf Rivers 1973). Freud does not associate the sexual instinct with the instinct to procreate because the former has no purpose beyond its gratification. Further, Freud considers genital sexuality desirable because it is a necessity and a fact. It cannot be suppressed or sublimated. Freud never accepts (genital) sexual continence as a fact of life, because it is incompatible with human nature. Genitality must manifest itself, whether in normal sexual acts or in dream hallucinations of sexual acts through "nocturnal pollutions" (Freud 1938: 608) or in substitutes like jokes or artistic acts. In Freud's view, a healthy person is the one who has "energetic sexual needs" and the capacity to fulfil them to his utmost satisfaction (cf Freud 1838: 615). The normal sexual act is coitus, and Freud's whole theory of sexual evolution in the child is based upon this idea of genitality as the highest stage of libido development (Freud 1938: 563 & Fromm 1970: 32).

Partly inherited and partly acquired, human sexuality, in Freud's view, is *species-uniform* and *species-specific*, that is *all* human beings, and *only* human beings, have sexual drives. Sexuality is a part of human destiny. Freud attaches so much importance to sexuality not only because it is the most ancient and the most dominant of human drives but also because it is highly flexible and prone to maldevelopment (cf Wollheim 1971: 123). To stress its peculiar nature, Freud calls it *libido* which has three characteristics: (i) it is the psychic energy that manifests sexuality (ii) it is a closed system regulated by the physical law of conservation of energy, so that libido withdrawn from one area must inevitably produce effects elsewhere and (iii) it passes through a chronological sequence to reach its climax in the form of adult genitality (cf Brown 1961: 22).

One of the most remarkable of Freud's contributions to the study of sexuality is his crucial distinction between what he calls the sexual *aim* and the sexual *object* (1938: 553-571). According to Freud, there are many forms of sexual behaviour which deviate from the norm in aim, or in object or in both and, yet, they are manifestations of sexuality. The normal sexual aim is coitus, and, the normal sexual object is a heterosexual adult partner. Deviations in aim constitute 'inversion' while deviations in object account for 'perversion' (cf Wollheim 1971: 110). An individual can see and obtain the realization of his sexual aim in such diverse forms as a partner of the same sex (homosexuality), his own body (autosexuality), anal movement (both retention and expulsion), oral involvement (viz kissing, biting, quarrelling, talking), causing pain to others (sadism) or to oneself (masochism), seeing or showing nakedness, love of pornography, dreams, jokes, slips, creative activities, gymnastics etc. Similarly, an individual can choose, for his sexual object, an adult of his own sex, a minor of the other sex, himself, an animal, a symbol, an idea, urine, faeces, dead bodies, inanimate objects and so on. Human ingenuity is nowhere as evident as in the domain of sexuality. Neither the sexual aim nor the sexual object nor the relationship between the two is a *constant*. The variability of *each* of them and the variability *between* the two of them make human sexuality a notoriously complex phenomenon. Freud makes it explicit in *The Three Essays on Sexuality* that no normal human being is without a streak of inversion and that no normal sexual act is without a tinge of perversion. "Even in the most normal sexual act", says Freud, "certain addenda are distinguishable, the development of which may lead to aberrations described as perversions" (1938: 563-64). He goes on to say, "the sexuality of most men shows an admixture of aggression, of the desire to subdue, the biological significance of which lies in the necessity of overcoming the resistance of the sexual object by actions other than mere *courting*" (p 569). When we condemn perversion, we must remember that "the highest and the lowest in sexuality are everywhere most intimately connected" (p 572). Morbid perversions such as "licking of faeces and the violation (i.e., raping) of cadavers" (p 571) are those specimens of human sexuality where an individual has overcome all resistances like shame, loathing, fear and pain. Each one of us, it should be remembered, has overcome such resistance to some extent.

Another remarkable contribution of Freud to the theory of sexuality is his formulation of the chronology of infantile erotic development (cf Freud 1938: 580-603), Brown 1961: 11-25, Wollheim 1971: 110-113 & Guerin *et al*, 1979: 129). Every child passes through a specifiable sexual evolution in a phased pattern: *oral*, *anal* and *genital*. The erotic development of the child is associated with certain orifices of the body: the mouth, the anus and the genitals. Each of these orifices has a dual function: (1) a vital somatic function and (2) a physically determined sexual function. These orifices perform certain basic, somatic functions like feeding, defecation and urination. Now, once any one of these functions is performed, the infant associates it with a pleasurable sensation and, once he experiences a pleasurable sensation, he likes to repeat it frequently. The child has an innate capacity to cause stimulation in his muscular system even without a psychological need and he has also the capacity to have a pleasurable sensation through his muscles at will. In course of time, the child develops his strategies to have pleasurable experiences even without a psychological function. The child's desire and competence to have a pleasurable sensation independent of a genuine psychological need and without a psychological function is the psychogenesis of infantile sexuality. Human sexuality has, thus, a psychic motivation and a somatic manifestation. Sexuality, with all its addenda and aberrations, is partly congenital to the human infant.

Combining the variability of aim and object and the various phases of the child's erotic development, Freud was able to arrive at the following generalizations: (i) adult sexuality is not necessarily heterosexual, (ii) coitus is not the only aim of sexuality, (iii) an adult partner is not the exclusive sexual object, (iv) sexuality, whether adult or infentile, is not necessarily a genital act and (v) sexuality does not solely depend on physical involvement.

The third premise of the Freudian paradigm relates to a certain psychic mechanism which is responsible for the stability of civilised existence as well as discontents. Throughout his life, man is confronted with an alternative, either total libidinous satisfaction and barbarism or partial libidonous satisfaction and cultural stability. As a member of a civilized community, man normally opts for the latter The exercise of this choice is effected by pushing back certain unacceptable ideas or impulses from the conscious into the unconscious, the reservoir of the libido and the domain of the id (cf Blum 1969: X & Wollheim 1971: 207). To this psychic mechanism Freud gave the name of *repression*. But once repression has taken place, the unfortunate human is again faced with an alternative : either perversion or *neurosis* (Freud 1963: 31 & Riviere 1973). An explanation of neurosis was seen by Freud as *the first task* of psychoanalysis (1938: 964). Since the basis of neurosis is repression, he devoted most of his time to formulating a theory of repression which was in his view the "pillar upon which the edifice of psychoanalysis rests" (p 939). In his history of psychoanalysis, Freud acknowledges his debt to three persons—Charcot, Breuer and Chroback (p 937) for the idea of the sexual basis of neurosis but he says that the theory of repression "I certainly worked out independently" (p 939). Freud was fully convinced that repression of a sexual wish is invariably the cause of neurosis (p 936). Freud did not believe in religion which was to him "an obsessional neurosis affecting the general mass of people" (Robert 1966: 296) and, as such, it was "baneful and eradicable" (Wollheim 1971: 220). Similarly, he did not accept continence as a fact of life; a common inference from his theory would be, to quote G M Gullen, that "absolute continence is unnatural and incompatible with mental health"

(Cioffi 1973). Since the libido operates according to the law of conservation of energy so that libido withdrawn from one area must inevitably produce effects elsewhere, Freud argues that sexuality permeates the whole of human life. One has either normal sexual acts or nocturnal pollutions 'through pleasurable dream hallucinations of a sexual act' (Freud 1938: 608), perversion or neurosis, sexual thrills or repressions. A character in an Aldous Huxley short story suggests to a woman that she should have sexual thrills rather than repressions: "Read Freud. Repressions are the devil" (cited in Cioffi 1973). Such a recognition of the ubiquity of sexuality leads Freud to a sort of pansexualism. Freud first identifies the psychic phenomenon with the expression of a wish or impulse, then the impulse with an unconscious or repressed impulse, then the repressed impulse with a sexual impulse and the conclusion is pansexualism. We take another route and arrive at the same conclusion: the mind is conceived as a system operating in accordance with the constancy principle, that is, accumulation of quantity leads to a tension and then there is an attempt on the part of the mind to rid itself of the tension, i.e., discharge of accumulated quantity, which is identified as sexual gratification (cf Wollheim 1971: 107). It seems plausible to argue that sexuality is the sole impulse of the mind irrespective of whether it is hunger versus sexual drive, id-instinct versus ego-instinct or Eros versus Thanatos. We have already seen that sexuality combines the highest and the lowest, attraction and loathing, nourishment and sexual gratification. The Freudian psychology is a study of neurosis which itself is a discovery of repression which is, in turn, sexuality diverted from its normal course. Whether one accomplishes the normal sexual act or has inversion, perversion or neurosis, each of which is partly congenital, one is always involved in sexuality. It is immaterial whether this involvement is wishful or compulsive, positive or negative, normal or neurotic, pregenital or genital, physical or psychic, real or symbolic. There are certain psychological formations which arise out of the mechanism of repression. These formations are: compromise solution, reaction-formation and sublimation. When repression takes place, there is often an agreement between the aggressive id and the appeasing ego/ superego that the demands of the former can be fulfilled in ways which do not interfere with the normal functioning of the individual. *A compromise solution* is a temporary truce between the sexual and the social/moral agents of the psyche so that the individual can maintain his public image and yet fulfil his sexual demands. An avowedly pacific person can thus condemn all forms of cruelty and yet remain absorbed with newspaper reports of sadism or with reading books on violence (cf Brown 1961: 7-8). Closely allied to such compromise solutions is *reaction-formation*, that is, a mechanism in which the forbidden drive is deflected to non-sexual aims and objects which are acceptable to the demands of cultural accomplishments. But as such formations are not genuinely sublimated, they give rise to the variety of contradictions in the life of the individual. It is not uncommon to come across a man who secretly sets a house on fire and later on joins other people to put out the fire. Exaggerated puritanism, excessive politeness and loud cries of helping the poor could be cited as some other examples of reaction formation. When the process of deflecting the sexual drive to non-sexual, socially acceptable, spheres of life is successfully completed, genuine *sublimation* can be said to have taken place. Sublimations are characterized by the smooth flow of pregenital drives towards alternative goals which are valuable to the standards of social morality and culture. Philanthropic activities and works of art could be seen as illustrations of complete sublimation which is a successful blending of creative ability, perversion and neurosis. Reaction-formation is a lower form of sublimation. It must, however, be noted here that, according to Freud, only pre-genital drives can be sublimated. Genital drives can change their form, aim and object but they can never be genuinely transformed or sublimated (cf Freud 1938: 625-26 & Brown 1961: 30). One of the aims of psychoanalysis is the transformation of pre-genital sexuality into genuine sublimation. This means that psychoanalysis also demands radical changes in the standards of existing sexual morality, if man is to maintain balance between civilization and his personal happiness.

**Theory of Dreams**

The most important contribution of Freud's theory of repression for the modern man has been to familiarize himself with the extent, variety and intensity of self-deceitfulness which he has so willingly harboured and nourished, often without having been aware of it. It was this theory that showed us that in each of us there has always been a deceiving principle, a lying activity, a constant, obstinate and ever-active tendency to camouflage ourselves in our own eyes as well as in those of others. Hyprocrisy is congenital to human consciousness (Riviere 1973). *The Interpretation of Dreams* is an encyclopaedic catalogue of the lies and distortions that pervade civilized existence. Freud clearly shows us that some of our dreams which appear to be obscure, incoherent and enigmatic are the most precious clues to the subtleties of our psychic life. These dreams baffle us because there is a gnawing discrepancy between their *manifest* content and *latent* content. Such dreams can best be seen as compromise solutions between the *repressed* impulses and the *censoring* agents of the mind (cf Riesman 1973 & Roazen 1973). Freud declares that all dreams are profoundly meaningful and absolutely truthful. *The dream,* says Freud, "is the disguised fulfilment of a suppressed or repressed wish" (1938: 235).

How do dreams succeed in disguising the fulfilment of a wish which was suppressed or repressed? To answer this question Freud charts out four technical processes which constitute the dream work. These processes are: (1) transformation, (2) condensation, (3) displacement and (4) symbolic representation (cf Freud 1938: 319-368 & Robert 1966: 114-125). The first process of the dream work *transforms* an idea into an *image* and a wish into a situation. Every dream must show the wish fulfilled in a *visual* form by transforming an abstract concept into images and situations. The second process, compresses or *condenses* the dream content so that people and objects acquire composite forms, often hybrid structures, due to the fusion of completely dissimilar features. The third process brings about a reversal or an exchange of the values involved. What was significant in real life becomes insignificant in the dream and vice versa. Nothing contributes more to the absurdity of dreams than this deceitful shift of emphasis brought about by *displacement*. Finally, the fourth process, replaces people, objects and situations by a closely knit network of symbols and images. This network delineates the dream content in a purely analogical fashion. This process which Freud calls *symbolism* (or symbolic representation) brings dreams closer to works of art and the dream work to artistic creation.

It has already been noted that only sexual wishes are repressed on account of their being unacceptable to consciousness and Freud therefore argues that dreams function only to fulfil those unsatisfied and repressed sexual wishes. But why do these fulfilments have to be camouflaged? As we all know, in waking life, the ego and the superego function to inhibit and repress undesirable drives (i.e., sexual drives). In dreams the agent of repression is the *censor*, the night-time representative of the ego and the superego. The dream censor is constantly at work and subtly takes charge of our "moral grooming" (Riviere 1973) even when we are asleep. This means that even in our dreams we are not entirely free from our reason or conscience, although the devil in us knows how to realize the goals. The dream, Freud holds, is an elaborate compromise, a final deal, between the devil and the custodian of nocturnal morality. Life, whether in sleep or in waking, is a series of such deals and compromises between sexuality and morality.

## IV

Freud never produced a systematic and complete exposition on the subject of literature or art. His pronouncements on the nature and function of art are available in the form of passing references and occasional remarks scattered throughout his major works. His views on specific works of art and artists are available in several brief essays like 'Delusions and Dreams', 'The Theme of three caskets', 'A childhood Recollection', 'Dostoevsky and Parricide', 'Leanardo da Vinci', and 'The Moses of Michael Angelo' (cf Robert 1966: 267-94, Morrison 1968: 233-36 & Fraiberg 1974: 10-44). If the scattered remarks in his books and the generalizations in his essays are gathered together, they will certainly constitute Freud's general analytic scheme of literature. But, there are two reasons why this is not done in this study. First, a thorough understanding of Freud's writings on literature would require a grasp of nothing less than the whole of psychoanalytic literature. Is it a reason for not trying to weave together all the threads of the Freudian thinking on literature? No. The reason for not trying to do so is very simple. Freud wrote his essays on literature, as he had written his major works, while carrying out his researches and therapies in psychoanalysis. He used examples from literature and art as illustrative material for his findings in psychoanalysis. Freud, perhaps, never analysed a work of art for a purely literary purpose. His assumptions and generalizations about art are those of a professional and committed psychoanalyst, not those of a literary critic, and, therefore, they display complete consistency with the principles and conclusions of psychoanalysis (cf Fraiberg 1974: 2).

### Freudian Paradigm of Literature

The second reason for avoiding the tedium of constructing an elaborate structure of the Freudian paradigm of literature is that most of his remarks and observations of theoretical significance are contained in his essay: 'Creative writers and Day-dreaming'. Unlike the other essays of Freud, this essay is not concerned with any specific work or artist. This essay can safely be taken as a general statement of Freud's theoretical position in respect of art or literature. It was in his *magnum opus* that Freud had equated the creative process with the dream work and with psychic formations like neuroses. The essay on 'Day-dreaming' is the most succinct account of the conceptual framework within which he analyses literature. It is obviously based on the broad framework within which the dream chapter work was analyzed in *The Interpretation of Dreams*. This study will, therefore, attempt to summarize and examine Freud's literary paradigm with special reference to these two texts. Terms like 'poetry', 'art' and 'literature', are being used here synonymously, as they are used in Freud's writings. The title of this chapter, therefore, could, without detriment to its theoretical position and conceptual clarity, easily have been 'the Freudian Paradigm of Art' or 'the Freudian Paradigm of Poetry'. It has already been clarified that this study does not claim to be an analysis of a paradigm of literature. It is a Freudian paradigm and, Freud's literary paradigm is not a literary paradigm in the sense in which Wordsworth's or Eliot's is. Within the Freudian frame of reference we have to look at literature through the eyes of a psychoanalyst and to treat literary criticism as integral, if not subservient, to the overall paradigm of psychic life. The central concern of this study is to examine and evaluate the adequacy of the psychoanalytic paradigm of literary criticism and, by extension, to examine this specific paradigm in such a way as to be able to deduce some verifiable conclusions about the adequacy of the psychic paradigm, as also about the validity of its generalizations. To his pleasant surprise, Freud discovered a parallel between his own work and the work of the poet, as far as the analysis of psychic mechanisms was concerned. "I have made use of this agreement between my investigations and the creations of the poet as a proof of the correctness of my method of dream-analysis" (1938: 189). Acknowledging his debt to creative writers for the methodological support he gathered from their works, Freud writes: "In psychic knowledge, indeed, they are far ahead of us, ordinary people, because they draw from sources that we have not yet made accessible for science" (cited in Fraiberg 1974: 7). The remaining part of this section will make it clear whether Freud praises creative writers for the right reasons or not.

Freud's literary paradigm seems to have been based on three assumptions:

(i) that it is theoretically valid and methodologically correct to deduce conclusions about the psychic life of artists on the basis of analyzing their works;

(ii) that a creative work, like a dream or a neurotic symptom, is unconsciously motivated; and

(iii) that a work of art is a disguised fulfilment of a suppressed or repressed sexual wish.

When we discuss Freud's method of discovering the psychic life of the poet through his poetry, we would recall Freud's classification of dreams into three categories. As dreams of the first category are left out of dream-analysis because they are simple and direct wish-fulfilments, likewise, overtly autobiographical or deliberately psychological works of art can be kept out of this sort of analysis because there is not much to psychoanalyze. Again, like the two latter categories of dreams, only those works are taken up by Freud for analysis in which the average reader does not suspect any hidden psychic determination. Most great works of art come within the purview of psychoanalytic investigation. A simple Freudian argument in support of such an assumption will be: since a work of art is a product of the poet's mind, it must have some causal connection to those psychic processes and mechanisms which motivated that work of art. Therefore, it is quite legitimate a procedure to discover 'facts' about the psychic life of the artist through the work of art. The work of art, Freud held, is the artist's psyche turned inside out. It is an externalized version of the poet's mind, whether he knows it or not, likes it or not.

M H Abrahms in his 'Preface' to *The Mirror and The Lamp* (1971) uses two antithetic but powerful metaphors of the mind to separate the romantic sensibility from the Augustan sensibility (in a sense, the entire traditional sensibility from the Platonic age to the last quarter of the eighteenth century): "One comparing the mind to a reflector of external objects, the other to a radiant projector which makes a contribution to the objects it perceives". The mind of the poet is a radiant projector which contributes to what it perceives and, in the process of contributing, lets off the secrets of its inner workings. Poetry, for many of the romantics, is "the overflow, utterance, or projection of the thoughts or feelings of the poet" (Abrahms 1071: 21). This way of thinking in which the artist himself becomes the major element "generating both the artistic product and the criteria by which it is to be judged", is called the *expressive* theory of art (p 22). For Freud, all art is expressive; all art reveals the unconscious of the mind (i.e., for Freud, they are near synonyms) of the artist. The work of art is a mirror to the private life of the poet. Nearly half a century ago, the eminent American critic, Kenneth Burke, propounded the view that only when a link was established between the work of art and the private life of the author could the work be fully understood and enjoyed. Biography, argues Burke, cannot be dismissed as irrelevant to the appreciation of art. As he puts it: "we can eliminate biography only if we consider the work of art as if it were written neither by people nor for people, involving neither inducements nor resistances" (1973: 285). He goes on to say, "It is possible to enjoy Coleridge's `The Ancient Mariner' without knowing anything about his personal life but if we knew Coleridge's addiction to opium we would better understand and enjoy the poem. The poem can be seen as a symbolic redemptive process" (p 281). Looking at the work-author relationship from the other end, Freud seeks to study works of art as concrete illustrations of the poet's psychic life, of the poet's unconscious motivations and mechanisms. As long as biography continues to be relevant to criticism, one might suppose that the psychoanalyst's search for clues and universal patterns in the work about the artist's motivational structure will remain important and interesting as a revealing or fact-finding tool of criticism.

Freud's occasional references to works and authors in his major writings and his essays on specific works and authors attempt to illustrate his assumption that the work of art has a logical correlation to the artist's psychic personality, his thinking and experiences. In his essay on Leonardo da Vinci, for instance, Freud tries to explain some of Leonardo's compositions with reference to his childhood experiences. Leonardo, Freud tells us, had two mothers. Catherina was his real mother who had abandoned him when she was very young and pretty and he was only a little child between three and five. Catherina had to abandon her son because he was an illegitimate child and because Leonardo's father had refused to marry her. Later on, Leonardo's father took him back but married another woman, Donna Albiera, who was also very young and beautiful and who also was full of love and tenderness for little Leonardo. Although, in later life, Leonardo never had any bitterness for either of his mothers, he found it impossible to get over the sense of ambivalence between his two loving mothers". Why did all this happen?, he could never explain to himself. Freud discovered a clear imprint of the double-faced, ambiguous mother in Leonardo's composition of 'Saint Anne'. Similarly, in the mysterious and blissful smile of 'Mona Lisa', Freud saw an image of Catherina when she was leaving Leonardo for ever: the smile of Mona Lisa ... had awakened in him as a grown man the memory of the mother of his earliest childhood" (Robert 1966: 288). In his essay on Dostoevsky, Freud draws some interesting conclusions about the novelist's personality, his passion for gambling and his epilepsy with particular reference to the theme of *The Brothers Karmazov*. Similarly, explaining the episode in Goethe's *Dictung Und Wahrheit* in which Goethe refers to his having thrown, as a young child, his parent's china out of the window, Freud interprets it as the little Goethe's aggressive reaction to the birth of a younger brother. (*A childhood Recollection*).

The second premise of the literary paradigm relates to the unconscious motivation of works of art. Freud's analysis offers a genetic explanation of artistic works. The work of art, Freud contends, could not have been all consciously planned and executed. The work therefore must refer to some specific compulsive force in the psyche which gave birth to it.

The unconscious motivation of human behaviour has already been discussed. Similarly, Freud's view of a work as an index to the poet's unconscious manoeuvering has just been discussed. We can therefore easily omit these two segments here and limit this part of the discussion to Freud's references to creative works as illustrative of certain universal psychic patterns. Freud does not always analyze a work of art to make revelations about the artist; sometimes, he turns to works of art because they contain clues about certain psychic formations and patterns which are universal and eternal. In *The Theme of Three Caskets*, for example, he explains how Shakespeare used the myth of three women (casket symbolizes woman) in two different ways. In *The Merchant of Venice* the theme is treated in the romantic context while in *King Lear* it is given a tragic turn. In Freud's view, Shakespeare chooses a myth in which the hero is faced with a choice among three women: the mother, the loving mate and the goddess of Death. In the *Merchant of Venice* the hero chooses the loving mate while in *King Lear* the hero is compelled to embrace the goddess of Death. Lear's carrying Cordelia's dead body on the stage is, for Freud, symbolical of man's ultimate reconciliation to the fact of death: "Eternal wisdom, clothed in the primeval myth, bids the old man renounce love, choose death, and make friends with the necessity of dying" (Robert 1966: 274). Similarly, Freud discovers a universal pattern in the Oedipus legend: "Fate and Oracle were no more than materializations of an inner necessity; and the fact of the hero sinning without his knowledge and against his intentions was evidently a right expression of his *unconscious* nature, of his criminal tendencies" (Fraiberg 1979: 9). Each human male, Freud believed, is an Oedipus, without his knowledge and against his intentions.

The central tenet of Freud's paradigm of literature is based on his perception of an undiminishing parallel between a neurotic formation (like a dream) and a work of art. Freud turns to a consideration of works and artists mainly because they provide ample support for his method and sufficient encouragement to his researches. In his *History of the Psychoanalytic Movement* he writes: "Very soon, it was discovered that the dreams invented by writers stand in the same relation to analysis as do genuine dreams. The conception of the unconscious psychic activity enables us to get the first glimpse into the nature of the poetic creativeness. The valuation of the feelings, which we were forced to recognize while studying the neuroses, enabled us to recognize the sources of artistic productions and brought up the problem as to how the artist reacts to those stimuli and with what means he disguises his reactions" (1938: 954). The *ars poetica* of the artist is the same as the technical processes of the dream work: transformation, condensation, displacement and symbolic representation. A creative work is just like a dream. Like the dreamer or the neurotic, the creative author chooses a way of communicating his own feelings which affords him the greatest degree of inner satisfaction. In psychoanalytic terms, this process assists the author "in maintaining internal balance by controlling levels of psychic tension and preventing them from shifting too rapidly or too far" (Fraiberg 1974: 30). The dreamer saves himself from pathological neurosis by letting off his tension through the dream; so does the artist through the artistic process. The artist, Freud therefore holds, is not a pathological neurotic but one who continually wavers on the threshold of neurosis, sometimes crossing it for the time being and then coming back to normality through the healing effect of his creations: "If the fantasies become overluxuriant and overpowerful, the conditions are laid for an onset of neurosis or psychosis". But the artist saves himself from such a catastrophe by articulating his fantasies in the form of a work of art (cf Freud 1972).

In his essay on "Day-Dreaming", while comparing the poet to a "child at play" (an epithet easily comparable to Thomas Love Peacock's description of poets as "the grown babies of the age" cf Wimsatt & Brooks 1964: 416), Freud points out that the only difference between the two is that while the child plays with concrete objects, the poet plays with his fantasies or illusions (play is opposed to reality and is hence an illusion). The poet is compelled to give up playing like a child because he is a grown man and a member of a respectable community. But the law of conservation of energy operates: we can never give up anything, we merely exchange one thing for another, and the poet has only exchanged infantile playing for adult day-dreaming. To quote Freud: "What appears to be a renunciation is really the formation of a substitute or surrogate" (1972). The poet makes his fantasies socially acceptable by his technique, his *ars poetica*. Extending this art-dream equation to primitive myths, Freud observes: "It is extremely probable that myths .... are distorted vestiges of the wishful fantasies of whole nations, the *secular dreams* of youthful humanity" (1972). It was really great that Freud saw the human mind as a poetry-making organ as Jung saw the human mind as a myth-creating or "mythopoeic" organ (cf Storr 1973: 32). Every man, says Freud, "is a poet at heart and... the last poet will not perish till the last man does" (1972). The poet, Freud would remind us, distinguishes himself from the rest of humanity only in *degree* and not in *Kind*. Freud is never oblivious of the simple fact that a work of art can be interpreted in a variety of ways. He only contends that even in respect of the capacity to admit of multiple interpretations a work of art is not very different from its allies like dreams and neuroses. In an interesting passage in *The Interpretation of Dreams* he observes:

"Just as all neurotic symptoms like dreams themselves, are

capable of hyper-interpretation, and even require such hyper-interpretation before they become perfectly intelligible, so every genuine poetical creation must have proceeded from more than one motive, more than one impulse in the mind of the poet, and must admit of more than one interpretation. I have here attempted to interpret *only* the *deepest substratum of impulses* in the mind of the creative poet" (1938:310-11 italics added). It is interesting to note that in Freud's view the multiplicity of interpretations that a work of art or a neurotic symptom may give rise to are not as important as Freud's deepest interpretation.

The pathological literalism of Freud's equation between creative activity and psyco-neurosis becomes more explicit when we turn to the third postulate of his literary paradigm. According to his fully-developed hypothesis, the etiology of psyco-neurosis depends on a triad of factors: frustration, fixation and conflict. The first two factors account for what Freud calls *perversion*, while the presence of the third ingredient along with the other two is responsible for a psychic formation called *neurosis*. Perversion, Freud tells us, occurs when the individual's libido has been frustrated at the level of genitality, has regressed to the more primitive level of the pregenital and is fixed there, while neurosis occurs when the libido has been frustrated at the genital level, has regressed to an earlier level and likes to be fixed there but some part of the individual's personality forbids the libido to secure satisfaction at the level to which it has regressed. The fixation-point may occur in respect of either the sexual aim or the sexual object. Moreover, since perversion has succeeded in obtaining fixation, the pervert is free from qualms of conscience. The neurotic is not free from psychic tension because his libido has not been allowed to stabilize or fix at the level to which it has regressed. This makes the neurotic a perpetually and restlessly *creative* individual. He is neither here nor there; continually wandering between two worlds: 'the one dead and the other yet unborn'. His libido has been frustrated at the level of genitality but it cannot stabilize at the pregenital level either, because the psychic watchman does not permit it to do so. The neurotic is therefore obliged to manifest his creativity in the form of certain symptoms which maintain his neurosis. It is crucial to Freud's argument to add that once an individual's libido had suffered frustration and has regressed to a safer stage, the individual is faced with alternatives: either to allow the libido to seek fulfilment at that stage or not to allow it; permission would bring perversion, and negation neurosis: "neurosis is the negative of perversion" (cf Freud 1938: 575; Freud 1971 and Wollheim 1971: 140-41). In Freud's view, the poet is neither a pervert nor a total neurotic. The pervert is a fully contented individual because he has succeeded in converting his genital frustration into pre-genital fixation. On the other hand, the neurotic is a perpetually restless individual because he has not succeeded in bringing about a conversion of his genital frustration into the pre-genital stability of fixation. The neurotic's *creativity* is manifested in the chain of pathological symptoms which he continually displays. The poet, like the dreamer, shares the genital frustration of the neurotic but he does not share the pathological symptoms because he has succeeded in drawing satisfaction of his libido from his fantasies. The creative process, therefore, is a psychic necessity for the poet as the dream-process is for the dreamer. As the dreamer saves himself from a total neurosis by obtaining fulfilment of his libido from his dream, the poet saves himself from total neurosis by drawing his libidinous gratification from his creativity. The creative process for the poet, like the dream process for the dreamer, is a means of drawing substitute gratification.

**Unsatisfied Wishes**

Every creative work is a disguised fulfilment of the poet's repressed or hidden sexual wishes. The poet is obliged to disguise the fulfilment of his sexuality for the same reasons for which he had to repress it. Social and moral values cannot allow a reasonable human being to satisfy his sexual wishes openly. But the fact remains that the motive forces of creative works are *unsatisfied wishes* and that every single fantasy is the "fulfilment of a wish, a correction of unsatisfying reality" (Freud 1972). The poet may have unsatisfied wishes of various sorts but his basic wish is a sexual wish. The motivating wishes of the poet are "either ambitious wishes, which serve to elevate the subject's personality; or they are erotic wishes ... but they are often united" (ibid). Why does the poet take to fantasy-making? Freud's answer is: "The artist is one who is urged on by instinctive needs which are too clamorous; he longs to attain to honour, power, riches, fame, and the love of woman, but he lacks the means of achieving these gratifications. So, like any other man with unsatisfied longing, he turns away from reality, and transfers all his interest, and all his libido too, on to the creation of his wishes in the life of fantasy" (cited in Read 1974: 425). In a similar passage, Freud says again: "The artist is originally a man who turns away from reality because he cannot come to terms with the demand for the renunciation of his instinctual satisfaction as it is first made, and who then in phantasy-life allows full play to his erotic and ambitious wishes" (cited in Wellek and Warren 1963: 82). It was due to the demand for the renunciation of instinctual gratification that the poet had, in his childhood, repressed his sexual wishes and it is because of a similar demand being now made that he is obliged to hide his modus of sexual satisfaction; "on the one hand, he knows that he is expected not to go on playing or fantasying any longer, but to act in the real world; on the other hand, some of the wishes give rise to his fantasies which are of a kind which it is essential to conceal" (1972). What is the secret of the emotional effect of a work of art on the audience? Moral, aesthetic and other considerations contribute to the total effect of a work of art, but, in Freud's view, the most important factor is the artist's success in arousing in his audience the same inner satisfaction which the fulfilment of the creative process has already brought to him. What the artist aims at is "to awaken in us the same emotional attitude, the same mental constellation as that which is produced by the impetus to create" (Fraiberg 1974: 37). The true enjoyment of literature, Freud argues, is relatable to "the release of tension in our minds" and the artist further intensifies such enjoyment by putting us into a position in which "we can enjoy our own day-dreaming without reproach or shame .... the essential *ars poetica* [of the poet] lies in the technique of overcoming the feeling of repulsion in us .... he bribes us through the purely formal—that is aesthetic—yield of pleasure which he offers us in the presentation of his fantasies. We give the name of *an incentive bonus* or a *forepleasure* to a yield of pleasure such as this..... It may even be that not a little of this effect is due to the writer's enabling us thenceforward to enjoy our own day-dream without self-reproach" (1972). Freud's account of the emotional appeal of a work of art comes very close to Coleridge's assertion: "The willing suspension of disbelief constitutes poetic faith" (Fraiberg 1974: 39). Accounting for the unique fascination of the *Oedipus Rex* of Sophocles in which Oedipus kills his father and marries his own mother, Freud observes: The fate of Oedipus "moves us only because it might have been our own" (1938: 308). In Freud's view, the extraordinary appeal of Shakespeare's *Hamlet* is due to the same reason, though in this play the Oedipal situation is rather repressed (or covert), but so is the Oedipal impulse repressed in each one of us (cf p 309). Ernest Jones confirms Freud's account of *Hamlet's* undiminishing appeal to all people and all ages in these words: "the hero, the poet, and the audience are all profoundly moved by feelings due to a conflict of the source of which they are unaware" (Jones: 1974).

## V

It may not be altogether unfruitful to study Freud's writings as a collection of pungent satires on contemporary Victorian society and its hypocritical ways. Like a true satirist, Freud seems to have fully exploited the gnawing discrepancy between appearance and reality with a view to exposing hypocrisy. He seems to have been fully conscious of the difference between the openly vicious and the hypocritical. Freud, perhaps, knew quite well that "the hypocrite's skin is notoriously more tender than that of the openly vicious. The one has nothing to conceal, the other everything. His whole reputation is at stake. Openly he subscribes to the ideals that secretly he ignores or defies" (cf Pollard 1970: 3). Freud may not have condemned the human race as *a race of the odious vermin,* as Swift had done, but he could easily have shared the satire that pervades many of Shaw's writings. In *Man and Superman* a meeting takes place between a brigand (Mendoza) and a gentleman (Tanner) and this is how they greet each other:

*Mendoza*: I am a brigand: I live by robbing the rich.

*Tanner*: I am a gentleman: I live by robbing the poor. Shake hands. (Shaw 1946: 114).

A little later, Mendoza tells Tanner: "A movement which is confined to philosophers and honest men can never exercise any real political influence: there are two few of them. Until a movement shows itself capable of spreading among brigands, it can never hope for a political majority" (p 117). Freud aimed at exposing these brigands who constituted political majority but, who looked like *gentlemen* in his age, and perhaps, in every other age and society. It is these brigand-gentlemen who openly condemn the Devil but secretly allow him to *reign in their hearts* (cf ibid, p 134).

Freud's life-long preoccupation (to the point of being obsessive) with *repression, neurosis* and the *Id* (a term ultimately derived from Nietzsche's *das Es* but borrowed from Georg Croddeck cf Wollheim 1971: 176) can best be seen as rooted in his historical sense and as an outcry against the empty moralizings of the hypocritical Victorian bourgeoisie. *The Freud,* says Eric Fromm, "who opened the way to the understanding of false consciousness was a radical thinker ... who transcended the limits of his society" (1970: 16). Whatever be the merit of his overall paradigm or of its specific concepts, Freud's thinking in its totality will certainly convince every conscientious and unbiased scholar of his incontestable intellectual honesty and moral earnestness. In Plato's account of the three parts of the soul, the best part is said to be that which "knows and loves knowledge" (Richards 1966). Allowing the best part of his soul the necessary degree of freedom, if a scholar were to study Freud against his historical background, he would, in all likelihood, come to the inevitable conclusion that Freud's most significant contribution to the history of ideas has been a purely *philosophical* one (of course, using 'philosophy' in the sense of 'love of wisdom'). Looking at Freud from this point of view, one is naturally reminded of Kant's unforgettable tribute to Hume: "The scepticism of Hume roused me from my dogmatic slumber" (cf Chatterjee & Datta 1960: 67). Rephrasing this statement one could very aptly say that 'The scepticism of Freud roused the Victorians from their dogmatic slumber'. The entire corpus of Freud's researches and writings could be fruitfully seen as a saga of his ceaseless attempts to awaken his age to its conscience.

From all that has been said so far, it must have become very clear that Freud was a great genius: a creative thinker and a powerful writer. It is therefore highly probable that one may never be absolutely right about him. But these two constraints need not push us into believing that all of Freud's hypotheses and conclusions are beyond question. It would really be too uncritical to accept Freud's generalizations about psychic life and its manifestations as indisputable theorems. The remaining part of this chapter attempts to offer a brief critique of the Freudian paradigm, both of psychic life and of literature. It has already been pointed out that, as Freud's theory of literature is just an illustrative extension of his theory of the mind, it is not theoretically valid to separate his paradigm of literature from his paradigm of psychic life in general and, therefore, such a separation, as proposed in this chapter, must be taken only as a mental abstraction for the limited purpose of this discussion.

However, it must be made clear that as his literary paradigm is included in his general psychoanalytic paradigm, it is quite legitimate to evaluate the latter so as to evaluate the former.

Freud's paradigm of literature has two obvious but crucial limitations: (i) its simplistic equations and (ii) its pathological bias. The first limitation relates to two important sets of equations between (i) the work of art and the psychic life of the artist and (ii) the work of art and the unconscious. The second limitation concerns Freud's negativistic approach to literature which arises, again, out of an assumed equation between a work of art and potential neurosis. These two limitations have serious and far-reaching consequences on Freud's basic understanding of literature. A great genius as he was, Freud could have, with his scholarship and sensitivity, constructed a powerful paradigm within which numerous historic researches could have been carried on for the benefit of literary scholarship, had he decided to study and analyze literature for its own sake and in its own terms, and independently of his professional loyalties. It was really unfortunate that such a wonderful mind allowed its vision of literature to be clouded by such extraneous considerations and constructs as those of psychoanalysis. Freud seems to have believed that a work of art is an adequate and authentic record of the artist's psychic life. Every student of literature knows that a work of art, howsoever great it may be, does not necessarily represent the truth of the artist and the man is often irrelevant to the work. Eminent poets and critics have been saying that the work of art is and should be independent of the man. Such poets and critics do not visualize any logical connection between the work of art and the private world of the man whose name is associated with the work. In his well-known essay on 'Tradition and the Individual Talent', T S Eliot remarks: 'The emotion of art is impersonal' (1953). In Eliot's view the greatness of an artist depends upon his capacity to transcend the personal and the private: "the more perfect the artist, the more completely separate in him will be the man who suffers and the mind which creates" (ibid). As far as the work is concerned, Eliot holds, the artist is without a personality: "the poet has not a 'personality to express, but a particular medium, which is only a medium and not a personality" (ibid). Eliot goes on to add, "Impressions and experiences which are important for the man may take no place in the poetry, and those which become important in the poetry may play quite a negligible part in the man, the personality" (ibid). That the poet is only a medium and not a personality is granted even by Plato. In *The Ion*, Socrates observes: "God takes away the minds of poets and uses them as his ministers, as he also uses diviners and holy prophets, in order that we who hear them may know them to be *speaking not of* themselves who utter these priceless words in a state of unconsciousness, but that God himself is the speaker, and that *through them* he is conversing with us" (Daiches 1956: 7 italics added).

"The character of the poet", Keats once wrote, "is to have no *self*, it is everything and nothing .... It has as much delight in conceiving an Iago as an Imogen ... A poet is the most unpoetical of any thing in existence, because he has no Identity —he is continually informing and filling some other body" (Wellek & Warren 1963: 60). The poet's mind, also said Keats, "is a thoroughfare for all thoughts" (Trilling 1980: 29). Jung begins his essay on `Psychology and Literature' with the preliminary remark that although a work of art is a product of complicated psychic activity, it is a product that is clearly "intentional and consciously shaped" (1972). It is, Jung argues, quite possible to draw inferences about the artist from the work of art, and vice versa; but these inferences are never compulsive; at best, they are "probable surmises or lucky guesses" (ibid). A viable theory of literature, Jung contends, cannot be constructed on the basis of such surmises and guesses that are only psychologically derived from the work of art, because, there is a fundamental difference between psychology and the study of art: "It is a principle in psychology that psychic events are derivable. It is a principle in the study of art that a psychic product is something in and for itself whether the work of art or the artist himself is in question. Both principles are valid in spite of their relativity" (ibid). For Jung, the artist, *as* an artist, is "an impersonal, creative process", a *work* and not *a human being*. The poet may go the way of "a Philstine, a good citizen, a neurotic, a fool, or a criminal. His personal career may be inevitable and interesting but it does not explain the poet" (ibid). There is no *symmetrical* implication between a work of art and the psychic life of the artist. To the majority of literary theorists, such as those quoted above, the relation between a work and its author's psyche is not even that of *asymmetrical* implication. Even if we granted that the work is related to the artist's psyche in the same sense in which a hyponym like 'rose' is related to a superordinate term like `flower', for the sake of the Freudian theory of art, the theoretical decision to use the work as a means of making generalizations, at the level of literary theory, about the artist's psychic personality is as absurd as to use a woman's smile to construct an indisputable biography of the woman's psychic totality. Freud does not seem to have understood the simple, fundamental fact that the poet's mind is geographically more extensive and structurally more complex than the totality of his works. It is, therefore, highly improper to attempt to read the poet's mind through a particular poem, even through a collection of poems. "To argue from *Hamlet* to Shakespeare's life and character", says David Daiches, "is a highly dubious procedure" (1956: 348). Similarly, I A Richards contends that "even if we knew far more than we do about how the mind works, to attempt to display the working of the artist's mind by the evidence of his work alone must be subject to the gravest dangers" (1960: 20). All this does not eliminate biography as a factor relevant to the study of literature. To use biographical information to understand or analyze a work of art is equivalent to looking at the work of art from the artist's personal life. Freud does not do this. He seeks to construct the psychic biography of the artist on the evidence of the work of art, which is tantamount to looking at the phenomenon from an entirely wrong end. Like the work-mind equation, Freud's equation of the work of art with the unconscious is another example of his strategic error. Freud does not find any difference between a creative work and a dream. It does not require one to be a psychologist to know that a work of art is fundamentally different from a dream, although it may have some superficial likeness to the dream. Dream is the work of a sleeping man, while a poem is made by the wakeful individual who may sometimes be *inspired*. At best, we can think of a creative writer as both 'maker' and `possessed', as combining "an obsessively held vision of life with a conscious, precise care for the presentation of that vision" (Wellek & Warren 1963: 85). Even the greatest works of art are, to a great extent, intentionally or consciously determined. The creative process, Freud should have realized, covers the whole gamut of activities, from the deepest unconscious motivations to the last conscious ramifications and revisions (cf Wellek & Warren 1963: 85 & Richards 1960: 20).

It is common knowledge that Freud began his career as a medical practitioner and remained in the medical profession till the last moment of his life and that psychoanalysis originated from Freud's commitment to his profession. But Freud's involvement in the medical profession had a very constricting effect on his understanding of the mind as well as on his perception of art. It was Freud's pathological bias that led him to equate the creative writer with a potential neurotic. It is a fact, as it should be, that a doctor spies out diseases, but it is "essential to the physician's art that he should not discover a disease where none exists" (Jung 1963). Any one who looks at art from the point of view of disease is bound to get a topsyturvy view of art, because art has its natural affinity with psychic health out of which it arises. An artist is the healthiest of human beings in the best sense of health. The basic problem with the Freudian perception of art emanates from his unfortunate shift from health to disease.

**Poetic Madness**

At this stage, when we are discussing Freud's equation of art with neurosis, it would not be out of place to briefly mention the notion of poetic *madness*, as it is known in literary criticism, with particular reference to Plato, Shakespeare and Dryden, in order to get a clearer view of the relativity of Freud's position. Plato, as we all know, wanted to keep the poet out of his ideal republic because the poet was a 'possessed' being who spoke in a divinely inspired frenzy. To Plato the poet's divine afflatus was a form of *madness* in a metaphoric rather than in a pathological sense. The Platonic poet, we must note, is something between a prophet and a mad man, sometimes the one, sometimes the other, and sometimes both. Poetic madness, says Plato in the *Phaedrus*, is "the madness of those who are possessed by the Muses; this enters into a delicate and virgin soul, and there inspiring frenzy, awakens lyrical and all other numbers" (Daiches 1956: 6). Plato held the view that a good poet is born, not made, and that good poetry is a revelation, not a making: "all good poets, epic as well as lyric, compose their beautiful poems not by *art* but because they are *inspired* and *possessed* .... For the poet is a light and winged and holy thing... [who utters] oracles" (The *Ion* cf Daiches 1956: 7, italics added). Plato's metaphoric use of 'madness' makes the term equivalent to 'genius' and genius is just the opposite of Freud's neurosis. Seneca was right when he said "there has been no great genius without some mixture of madness" (Dryden 1976: 50). Madness for Plato, as for Seneca, was not a sign of mental illness, as Freud thought it to be.

In *Absalom and Achitophel* Dryden somehow identifies poetic genius with madness in the following lines: "Great wits are sure to madness near ally'd/And thin partitions do their bounds divide" (p 18). This may be taken in two ways: either as an ironic statement about Achitophel, the villain, or as a metaphoric statement of that level of human experience at which the twin hemispheres of poetic genius and madness unite. For Achitophel, as for Zimri, "the blest mad man", madness is a neurotic formation, a disease, whereas for the poet *madness* is the sign of his superior psychic health. The two interpretations have two distinct focuses; but one thing is clear: what applies to the villain cannot apply to the poet.

It is quite a fashion among literary scholars to quote Shakespeare in support of the notion of poetic madness. A careful look at the following lines will, however, reveal that Shakespeare's comparison of the poet to a mad man and a lover is limited to a single dimension; the poet shares with the madman and the lover the gift of imagination; but the poet clearly distinguishes himself from the other two in his use of the gift of imagination:

"Lovers and madmen have such seething brains,
Such shaping fantasies, that apprehend
More than cool reason ever comprehends.
The lunatic, the lover, and the poet
Are of imagination all compact.
One sees more devils than vast hell can hold:
That is the madman. The lover, all as frantic,
Sees Helen's beauty in a brow of Egypt.
The poet's eye in a fine frenzy rolling,
Doth glance from heaven to earth,
and from earth to heaven,
And as imagination bodies forth,
The forms of things unknown, the poet's
Turns them to shapes, and gives to airy nothing
A local habitation and a name".

(*A Midsummer Night's Dream* V: 14-17, p 95).

The madman of these lines with a seething brain, which is full of the devil, is a mad man in the Freudian, pathological sense. But the poet is a mad man whose imagination is a shaping and creating one unlike the frantic imagination of the lover or the devilish one of the lunatic, and, therefore, the poet is either *not a madman* or a madman in the *holiest sense of the word*. The two madmen are as different as are creation and destruction, life and death, light and darkness or heaven and hell.

It may have become clear from the preceding paragraphs that madness is used by Freud in a literal sense while it is used in a metaphoric sense by Plato, Shakespeare and Dryden as far as the poet is concerned. The Freudian use is also pejorative as opposed to the highly complimentary use made of the word by literary men. Besides, there is a crucial difference between the two uses, a difference of emphasis. For literary men madness is an analogy of creativity while, for Freud, creativity is an analogy of madness. Borrowing the technical terminology of I A Richards (cf 1965: 117) one could better emphasize the fundamental difference between the two uses of madness. In literary circles, madness is the *vehicle* while creativity is the *tenor* but in Freudian literature creativity is the vehicle while madness is the tenor. For Freud poetic creativity is illustrative of neurosis while for literary men madness is a proof of poetic creativity at its highest. As the two approaches have diametrically opposed emphases, the two uses of madness do not share the same *ground* (i.e., ground in the Ricardian sense).

Freud's pathological bias inevitably led him to formulate a theory of literature which was ultimately to become, what Jung calls, *unduly negativitic* (cf Roazon 1973). It was this bias that did not allow him to visualize literature as a powerful way of enhancing man's grip on reality (cf Storr 1973: 31). It was this bias that pushed Freud into developing a sort of critical *monism* which reduces every work of art to a disguised fulfilment of an unsatisfied and repressed sexual wish. Freud never realized that meaning in literature is generally *context-sensitive* rather than *context-free*, at least, as far as non-archetypal symbols are concerned. As the same symbol may mean two different things in two works of the same author, it is not theoretically valid to read meanings into the psychic life of the poet through such symbols. As for archetypal images, it deserves to be noted that since they refer to timeless and universal patterns of psychic life, they cannot be interpreted with respect to the poet's personal life. Shakespeare may have used the myth of three women in *King Lear* and it was very insightful of Freud to have drawn attention to the possibility but, then, this is "not *the* meaning of *King Lear* any more than the Oedipus motive is *the* meaning of *Hamlet*" (Trilling 1970: 60). It was also Freud's pathological bias that made him develop a patronizing attitude to art. Freud nowhere spoke of the artist as a conscious creator of values or as one who could transcend the limits of time and place. The influence of the artist upon the age is not less than the influence of the age upon the artist. The artist is as much a leader as a spokesman of his age and society and he is looked upon with respect, sometimes with reverence and awe. But Freud always viewed art "as a modern city-planner views a zoo or a park, as a territory zoned off from the work-a-day world, which is there to delight but not to be taken with full seriousness" (Riesman 1973). Above all, Freud never realized that no amount of psychoanalyzing a work of art can tell us whether the work is good or bad (cf Daiches 1956: 341, 348). Psychoanalysis, even at its best, cannot offer a paradigm sufficient for critical evaluation of literary texts.

There are certain inherent flaws in Freud's model of the mind which militate against its scope, objectivity, clarity and theoretical sophistication. One can examine this model from any point of view: social, economic, theoretical, methodological, interpretive or any other but the inevitable conclusion remains the same, that is, Freud's model starts with sexuality and ends with sexuality. All the levels of his theory and all the components of the model rally round the frustration of the libido and its fall-outs. Freud's entire theoretical framework can easily be reduced to a bunch of concentric circles which have the common centre of unsatisfied libido. Neurosis, repression, id, ego, superego, psychic processes, behaviour patterns, complexes, inhibitions, fixations, compromise solutions, sublimations, dreams, jokes, slips, works of art, creativeness, destruction, love, hate, peace, war, life and death are motivated by the unsatisfied libido and directed to the satisfaction of the libido, howsoever, invisible or oblique, these motivations and directions may be. Freud's general paradigm of psychic life, full of vulnerable hypotheses and dogmatic generalizations as it is, can be criticized on a number of grounds, some of which are discussed below:

(a) A number of sociological, economic and interpretive biases characterize Freud's approach to the theme of sexuality. Freud's theory of sexuality is determined by what Fromm calls a *patri-centric acquisitive culture*, that is, a culture which is economically sound and in which the male is the only authority, the real patriarch (cf Fromm 1970: 19, 58, 61, Burke 1973: 272-73 & Storr 1973: 8). Freud's culture is a culture in which every one has enough food so that he can easily afford to think about and satisfy his infinite sexual needs. But this is not the case with a hungry man. It would rather be blasphemous to talk about the sexual needs of a starving man. Again, Freud's culture is a culture of the neo-patriarch to whom the woman is a helpless sexual object, because she is an unfortunate, crippled and castrated male, and the child (whether male or female) is the sole property of the 'man-father' and nothing of the 'woman-mother'.

Psychoanalysis is based on the reports of the patients who display their inner world through the technique of *free-association* and the interpretations of these reports by the therapist. Since psychoanalysis has to depend upon such patient-therapist interactions, the entire technique may be coloured by what Blum (1969: 21-22) refers to as *interpreter bias* and *patient bias*. The therapist's professional training, his own psychoanalysis and his commitment to theory can easily affect his interpretations and the generalizations which arise out of them. Similarly, the patient can be influenced by his personal factors, his attitude to the therapist and, above all, his tendency to produce material conforming to the latter's theoretical expectations.

Now, a theory which is inhibited by so many factors cannot claim much objectivity and clarity.

(b) The second disturbing aspect of Freud's analytic scheme is its paucity of data and hurried generalizations. Rules Romain legitimately charges the conceptual framework of Freud with scientific levity; there is a marked and consistent tendency in Freud to transform his hypotheses into laws without having gathered the quantity of experiments and objective proof that are necessary for a scientific hypothesis (cf Riviere 1973). Similarly, Riviere has strong reservations about the validity of Freud's conclusions: "when we read Freud, we are struck by the rapidity of certain of his conclusions. Very often we see him making an affirmation which he has immediately generalized from a single fact that he reports; very often, too, if he is able to interpret a fact along the line of theory, he seems to find this sufficient to exclude any other interpretation" (1973). Freud's obsessive commitment to the central tenet of sexuality leads to affirmations which are dogmatic. *All* of Freud's conclusions, not *some* of them (as Riviere holds), turn out to be dogmatic, because all his hypotheses and generalizations seek to confirm his basic hypothesis that the mind is just sexuality and nothing else. It is this obsession of Freud that makes his interpretations artificial and his affirmations empty. The Freudian theory of mind, argues Jung, has "the rigidity of a dogma and the fanaticism of an inquisitor" (1973). It is Freud's obsession with sexuality that so severely limits the scope of his paradigm of psychic life. A model which is limited to a particular fraction of the phenomenon cannot achieve the status of an adequate paradigm. Flashes of insight couched in eloquent verbalizations cannot, by themselves, constitute a paradigm in science, howsoever readable and enjoyable these verbalizations may be.

(c) The third weakness of the psychic model proposed by Freud is its never-ending dualism. The human mind is perpetually torn between two warring factions: sex versus hunger, id versus ego, Eros versus Thanatos, till it is reduced to total extinction by the victory of the Thanatos over the Eros.

Freud cannot visualize any possibility of the mind's capacity to transcend its duality: tension and release, accumulation of quantity (or Q) and discharge followed by a new sequence of tension-release, accumulation-discharge, until the repetition compulsion takes the mind to the inorganic state. Thus, within the Freudian frame of reference, there is either opposition or annihilation, but no reconciliation or integration. Freud uses a fine word, *sublimation,* to describe the individual's passage from the pregenital pursuits to the socially acceptable modes of behaviour but it is distressing that he does not include in this concept the idea of the mind's innate capacity to transcend all its dualities, including that of sexuality (i e., tension and release). If the supreme goal of the Freudian *maturation* process were the attainment of *integration* or *wholeness* (as it was of Jung's *individuation* process cf Storr 1973: 87 & 103), *sublimation* could be said to have been used with real insight and justification. As it stands, Freud's sublimation is a very suggestive term but a vacuous concept. The vacuity of the concept emanates from Freud's partial view of sexuality. Freud never realized that the highest aim of psychic life, including all creative activities and spiritual pursuits, is the attainment of stability and wholeness. Had Freud realized this, psychoanalysis could have accounted for psychosynthesis and could have become the German parallel of Indian Yoga (cf Jung 1963: 63). Yoga in India accounts for psychosynthesis in terms of stabilization of consciousness at its centre. If consciousness makes a centripetal movement towards the kingdom of the mind, and finally succeeds in settling itself upon the centre, it achieves spiritual ecstasy. The centripetal movement of consciousness and the culmination of this movement in the form of psychic stability is beautifully described in a number of verses in the *Geeta* (cf II: 55-72). We can, for example, quote verse 55 which says:

*Prajahati yada kaman*
*Sarvan partha manogatan,*
*Atmanyevatmannatushtah*
*Sthtaprajnastadochyate.*

When consciousness has abandoned all centrifugal movements (i.e., desires) and their corollaries (i.e., attachment to objects), and is delighted in the self, it is said to have reached stability or sublimation.

(d) A major drawback of the Freudian model is its obstinate denial of psychic pluralism, both in respect of motivation and the realization of goals. Freud's model is a model of sexualization: whatever man does, he does because of, and, for sexuality. All human motivations, pursuits, purposes and executions are of, by, and for, sexuality. Man is an embodiment of the libido. From birth to death, from phallus to philanthrophy, from earth to heaven, and from the finest chord in the psychic motivation to the grossest manifestation of behaviour in the external world, man is either pining for or pacifying the libido monster. This is the Freudian paradigm of psychic life. This is a paradigm in which everything is reduced to sexuality which is co-terminus with psychic life in general or, with human behaviour in general, and, above all, with human existence as such. This is Freud's reductionism. This is what Burke calls Freud's *essentializing strategy* (1973: 261). Burke holds the view that every reduction is a simplification and that every simplification is an *over-simplification* (cf ibid, p 262). One of the finest examples of over-simplification is Freud's implicit view that the only relationship which obtains and can sustain between a human male and a human female (whether father-daughter, mother-son, or brother-sister) is a genital union. Another specimen of Freudian oversimplification is an unqualified equation between psychic formations like hysteria, neurosis, psychosis, inversion, perversion, etc and the frustration of the libido. There are, however, psychoanalysts who do not agree with such sweeping generalizations. Eric Fromm, for example, questions Freud's interpretation of the child-mother relationship in terms of sexuality on the ground that the child's tie to the mother is *common to both boys and girls* (1970: 19). Similarly, Jung explains the psychogenesis of neurotic formations with reference to the individual's loss of sense in the meaning of existence. Jung contends that neurosis is an *existential* rather than a sexual problem (cf Storr 1973: 42 & Fromm 1970: 49). In *The Dynamics of Creation*, Storr accounts for the restless creativity of the child by relating it to the 'intrinsically frustrating' experiences of childhood, the child is restlessly creative because he is continually searching for *ideal solutions* in the various spheres of his life and not because he is prompted by his sexual drives (cf Storr 1973: 43). Jung goes to the extent of refuting the very basis of the hypothesis of infantile sexuality. Scientifically, argues Jung, "the theory of sexuality of the suckling has little value. It is a matter of indifference to the caterpillar whether we say of it that it eats its leaf with ordinary pleasure or with sexual pleasure" (1973). Moreover, Freud's chronology of the infantile erotic development is alarmingly regressive, backward-looking: "His only interest lies where things come from, never where they are going" (cf Jung 1973).

There is no consensus among psychologists on whether the libido is the most dominant motivating force in the mind. According to Adler the dominant motive is the will-to-power, while according to Jung and D H Lawrence it is the *spiritual* instinct (cf Evans 1964: 34, 35, 69 & 80, Storr 1973: 65 & 117, & Morrison 1968: 204-205). The relative superiority of an impulse in the hierarchy of impulses is determined by a number of variables *viz* social, economic, political, cultural etc. There cannot be *any one* motive to claim dominance or priority throughout geography and history. By denying the relativity of motivation and goal-realization, Freud drastically narrows down the theoretical scope of his paradigm.

Freud's interpretation of dreams, jokes, slips and works of art in terms of neurotic formations is disappointingly artificial and tediously dogmatic. Wittgenstein was absolutely correct in his evaluation of Freud's interpretation of dreams: "To learn from Freud you have to be critical, and psychoanalysis generally prevents this" (1973). There are different sorts of dreams as there are different sorts of work of art, jokes and slips, and, there cannot be a single line of explanation for all of them. Some dreams like some jokes, slips and works of art, are wishfulfilments in the typical Freudian sense but it is simply *absurd* to hypothesize that *all* dreams and *all* works of art are disguised fulfilments of the unsatisfied libido. Kenneth Burke makes an interesting observation in this connection: "Freud characterizes the dream as the fulfilment of a wish; an opponent shows him a dream of frustration, and he answers: "But the dreamer wishes to be frustrated" (1973: 272).

Wittgenstein's remarkable comment on the interpretive reductionism of Freud exposes the inherent vulnerability of the system: "compare the question of why we dream and why we write stories. Not everything in the story is allegorical. What would be meant by trying to explain why he has written just that story in just that way?

There is no one reason why people talk. A small child babbles often just for the pleasure of making noises. This is also one reason why adults talk. And there are countless others" (1973).

(e) The crucial limitation of the Freudian model is its unflinching faith in the universal validity of the law of psychic determinism. Every child (boy or girl) is born of a mother, has a father, has to grow up, attain independence and win a mate. The boy differs from the girl only in that the former chooses the mother, while the latter turns to the father, for sexual fulfilment. This is Freud's picture of a *given*, (not a *taken*) reality, which is fixed and static, and, to which every boy and every girl have to conform. This picture denies the greater truth of a taken, dynamic reality which is determined by a number of socio-cultural and historical factors. Man's spiritual ecology and his intellective-emotive preferences are shaped more by cultural variations than by his biology. The maturation (or individuation) process differs from culture to culture and from age to age. Freud's law of causality does not take these variations into account. It does not, perhaps, cannot, account for individual variations. If a theory of the mind treats *all* human beings as exactly alike and all human beings of a particular age as exactly like those of another, then such a theory falsifies itself and has no claim to any degree of scientificness. As a matter of fact, there are only a few *constants* in psychic life; it is the variables of the milieu and the moment which largely constitute the extremely complex phenomenon known as the 'human mind'. The Freudian paradigm is based on an indefensible mechanization (or computerization) of the human psyche and it is, therefore, not a scientific paradigm. It is not *science*, it is *mere scientism* or perhaps, *sheer occultism*, an ally of numerology and the like.

There are eminent psychologists, philosophers and scientists who attach great importance to the fact of variations in the psychic behaviour of human beings. To illustrate this point we can quote a few. That there is no one-to-one correspondence between stimulus and response is attested by a number of scholars. Jung, for example, says:

"Coming to a brook, one person will say he jumps it for fun; another, because there is no alternative; a third because every obstacle challenges him, a fourth does not jump it, because he hates useless efforts, a fifth refrains from it because he saw no urgent necessity, a sixth because he lacks confidence; a seventh because his knees are rheumatic, and so on. My profession has always forced me to take account of the *peculiarities* of individuals" (cited in Das 1949: 165, italics added). Swami Vivekananda once said humourously: "If you and I and all who are present here were to think exactly the same thoughts, there would be no thoughts for us to think.... *variation* is the sign of life, and it must be there" (1964: 397). In his *Guide to Science* Isaac Asimov contrasts the exquisite structure of the spider's web with the imperfection of a human creation in the following lines:

"Looking at the spider's intricate web, built with beautiful precision and effectiveness for the function it will serve, it is almost impossible to believe that the thing has been done without purposeful intelligence, yet the very fact that the complex task is carried through so perfectly and *in exactly the same way* every time is itself proof that intelligence has nothing to do with it. Conscious intelligence, with hesitations and weighings of alternatives that are inherent in deliberate thought, will give rise to *imperfections and variations* from one construction to another" (1975: 392, italics added).

Similarly, an eminent philosopher of science, Thomas Kuhn, makes the following remark on this topic:

"If two people stand at the same place and gaze in the same direction ... we are under no obligation to suppose that the sensations of our two viewers are the same. On the contrary, much neural processing takes place between the receipt of a stimulus and the awareness of a sensation. Among the few things that we know about it with assurance are: *that very different stimuli can produce the same sensation; that the same stimuli can produce very different sensations*; and finally that the route from stimulus to sensation is in part conditioned by education. Individuals raised in different societies behave on some occasions as though they saw different things" (1970: 192-193, italics added).

Finally, the view taken in this chapter is that Freud's so-called theory of the mind does not, and cannot, have the status of a scientific paradigm and that this theory has nothing profitable to literary criticism at the level of theory construction. No viable theory of literature can be constructed out of the collection of the profound insights and brilliant observations which abound in the writings of Freud. All this, however, does not deny the fact that Freud has made a difference to twentieth century thinking about the human mind in general and about literature in particular. Perhaps, the best and the briefest evaluation of Freud's contribution to the fund of knowledge is contained in the following lines of W H Auden's 'In Memory of Sigmund Freud':

"If often he was wrong, at times, absurd,
to us he is no more a person,
now but a whole climate of opinion,
Under whom we conduct our different lives".

(Auden 1973)

4

# The Jungian Mystique of Literature

Literary students of Jung are generally fascinated by his insight into and reverence for literature and literary artists. Unlike Freud, who reduces creativity into a form of neurosis, Jung elevates the creative gift to the level of an apotheosis, next only to man's sense of divinity. Disturbing it is that Freud never rises above his obsessive pathological bias against art and artists. Jung is perhaps right when he observes that the Freudian theory of art displays "the rigidity of a dogma and the fanaticism of an inquisitor" (1966: 39). Freud does not realize that art is the opposite of neurosis or that the study of art is radically different from the investigation of psychic disorders. Jung puts it beautifully: "A doctor naturally has to seek out the causes of a disease to pull it up by the roots, but just as naturally the psychologist must adopt exactly the opposite attitude towards a work of art" (*ibid* 71). Anyone who looks at art from the pathological point of view is bound to shift from health to disease. It is true that the artist is at times compared to a mad man even by artists themselves. Shakespeare equates the poet with the *lover* and the *lunatic,* while Dryden places him next to the madman: "Great wits are sure to madness near ally'd,/And thin partitions do their bound divide" (quoted in Sharma 1986). But here we must be careful to separate the artist's use of madness from the Freudian use of neurosis. For literary men madness is an analogy of creativity, while for Freud creativity is an analogy of neurosis. Freud's art-neurosis equation can easily be dismissed on the basis of commonsense, for the artist is, by all standards, the healthiest of men in the best sense of 'health'.

Though it is sometimes possible to establish a direct link between the material of a work of art with the very private experience of the artist in the same way that there is a connection between a neurotic symptom and the very private experience of the neurotic, it cannot be supposed that the work of art and the neurotic symptom must have the same explanation. If a work of art is explained in the same way as a neurosis, then, Jung tells us, "either the work of art is a neurosis or neurosis is a work of art. This explanation is all very well as a play on words, but sound commonsense rebels against putting a work of art on the same level as a neurosis. An analyst might, in an extreme case, view a neurosis as a work of art through the lens of his professional bias, but it would never occur to an intelligent layman to mistake a pathological phenomenon for art, in spite of the undeniable fact that a work of art arises from much the same pathological condition as a neurosis" (1966: 67). Unless the analyst is cautious, the psychoanalysis of a work of art will fail to identify and display the subtle nuances of the work of art and the temptation to draw daring conclusions may easily lead to flagrant abuses. As Jung puts it: "A slight whiff of scandal often leads spice to a biography, but a little more becomes a nasty inquisitiveness—bad taste masquerading as science. Our interest is insidiously deflected from the work of art and gets lost in the labyrinth of psychic determinants, the poet becomes a clinical case and, very likely, yet another addition to the curiosa of *psychopathia sexualis*" (*ibid*, p 68). The technique of psychoanalysis strips the work of art of its unique beauty with the result that the "golden gleam of artistic creation—the original object of discussion—is extinguished" and so it "must be broken down and the way cleared by healthy adaptation" (*ibid*, p 69). In order to do justice to a work of art, the psychological approach must rid itself entirely of its medical prejudice, for a work of art is not a disease and therefore it requires an approach very different from the pathological one.

Freud's negativistic or reductionistic approach to literature is bad enough but what irritates the literary-minded still more is his patronizing and dismissive attitude to the whole profession of art and literature. He views art, a critic rightly remarks, "as a modern city-planner views a zoo or a park, as the territory zoned off from the work-a-day world, which is there to delight but not to be taken with full seriousness" (Riesman quoted in Sharma 1986). As opposed to this, Jung shows a much healthier attitude to art and a far superior understanding of its structure, nature and function and it is these factors that account for the greater influence and usefulness of his theories to the practice of literary criticism.

**Jung's Views on Intellect**

Jung's depreciation of the intellect need not be misconstrued as a plea for anti-intellectualism. He is all praise for the splendid empirical capacities of the intellect but he does not believe in the monopoly of the intellect. For him, unlike for Freud, natural science or rationalism is not enough (cf Storr 1973: 9). There are moments in life when our rationality, our intellect or our science fails us. When the temporal touches the permanent, our rationality cannot shape or articulate our experience. There is a way of knowing, experiencing and articulating that is more profound and reliable than the barely intellectual. For all its wonderful capacities, the intellect cannot generate to tap the primordial powers; it cannot give us what D H Lawrence calls *blood knowledge* or *bone knowledge*, that is knowledge gained when the whole person is actively involved in his world; it cannot, as Whitman puts it, "start with the sun" (cf Handy and Westbrook 1974). Literature, Jung believes, is a unique gift for man because it gives him a kind of knowledge which his science, his rationality or his intellect cannot give him. Jung, unlike his one-time mentor, readily endorses the claims of literature to embody knowledge, to celebrate sublime awareness, to distribute divine and eternal wisdom and to enlarge the human sensibility (cf Lodge 1972).

Jung strikes a note of radical departure from the Freudian creed when he invests the deeper layers of the unconscious with "shadowy symbolic forms" which represent for him "the collective wisdom of man's remote past" and upon which the individual can "draw and profit" (Woodworth 1965: 306). He lays down, with a sense of urgency, that the unconscious is "capable at times of assuming an intelligence and a purposiveness which are superior to actual conscious insight" and that certain dreams and myths are far more purposive, intelligent and significant than many conscious acts (cf Wimsatt & Brooks 1964: 716). The implications of this judgement are really very large for literary criticism. To attribute intelligence and purposiveness to dreams and myths and to declare that certain dreams and myths are more purposive, significant and intelligent than others clearly prepare a ground for a cognitive criticism and interpretation of dreams and myths. Jung means to tell us that the main function of such purposive, significant and intelligent dreams and myths which are, in fact, very elaborate symbolic structures and whose parts are ordered according to the "logic of the imagination", is knowledge-giving and knowledge-sharing: they give us knowledge of ourselves. It is this approach to myths and dreams that accounts for Jung's enormous and intimate impact on post-Freudian literary criticism. It is to Jung's credit that he brings a cognitive criticism to bear upon myths and dreams and, thereby, on works of art. With a pointed reference to Freud's disparagement of the so-called dream-facade, Jung remarks: "We say that a dream has a false front only because we fail to see into it. We would do better to say that we are dealing with something like a text that is unintelligible, not because it is a facade, but simply because we cannot read it" (*ibid*, p 717). In his autobiography he says that he cannot agree with the Freudian hypothesis that the dream has "a facade behind which its meaning lies hidden, a meaning already known but maliciously, so to speak, withheld from consciousness. To me dreams are a part of nature which harbors no intention to deceive, but expresses something as best as it can. These forms of life ... have no wish to deceive our eyes, but we may deceive ourselves because our eyes are shortsighted" (1967: 185).

Purged of its Freudian vices, the dream invites comparison to the work of art. "A great work of art", Jung writes, "is like a dream". And he specifies two ways in which it is: "for all its apparent obviousness it does not explain itself and is never unequivocal" and, like the dream, it requires us to make our own interpretation, for it presents an image "in much the same way as nature allows a plant to grow, and we must draw our own conclusions" (1966: 104). A great work of art is analogous to an elaborate, consistent and meaningful dream for it suggests a certain logic and a certain intention as the dream does. Moreover, like a great dream, a great work of art makes use of symbols and images which are remarkably public and traditional and not so private or clandestine as some people might think. Jung discovers a striking resemblance between the condensations, juxtapositions and symbolic ambiguities of great dreams and those of great works of art (cf *ibid*, p 717). Such dreams and works of art are comparable not only because they display a high degree of purposiveness and consistency but also because both of them defy and transcend the bounds of a purely rational interpretation.

**The Psychologist's and the Critic's Study of Literature**

Jung's emphasis on the analogy that certain dreams bear to certain works of art need not push us to the conclusion that there is a straight sort of parallelism between the two. He in fact draws a very sharp distinction between them. A dream, however purposive and significant it may be, is *entirely* shaped by the unconscious while a great work of art, even though it emanates from the inmost depths of man's being, is "apparently intentional and consciously shaped" (1966: 85). Besides, Jung draws a neat line of demarcation between a psychologist's study of literature and a critic's study of literature. The practice of art is, no doubt, a psychological activity and, as such, a fit subject for psychological investigation, but the very tools of psychology impose a very definite limitation on the psychological viewpoint. The psychologist can analyze only that aspect of art which consists of the process in artistic creation; he cannot analyze or judge that aspect of art which relates to its essential nature or constitutes its artistic value: "whatever the psychologist has to say about art will be confined to the process of artistic creation and has nothing to do with its innermost essence. He can no more explain this than the intellect can describe or even understand the nature of feeling" (*ibid*, p 66). A psychologist, *qua* psychologist, cannot determine the aesthetic value of a work of art because the study of art is not a subdivision of psychology even though psychology deals with the activity of the human brain (cf *ibid*, pp 65-66). Psychology and aesthetics do certainly have a common ground as far as the process of artistic creation is concerned but they can never replace each other as the former draws upon the principle of causality while the latter has a different set of values. As Jung writes: "It is an important principle of psychology that any given psychic material can be shown to derive from causal antecedents; it is a principle of aesthetics that a psychic product can be regarded as existing in and for itself. Whether the work of art or the artist himself is in question, both principles are valid in spite of their relativity" (*ibid*, p 87). Their respective standards of judgement are so different that the psychologist cannot hope to share the lens of the literary critic. "There is", says Jung, "a fundamental difference of attitude between the psychologist's approach to a literary work and that of a literary critic. What is of decisive importance and value for the latter may be quite irrelevant for the former. Indeed, literary products of highly dubious merit are often of the greatest interest to the psychologist" (*ibid*, pp 87-88). Above all, what most separates psychology from literary criticism is the question of meaning. Psychology is a continuous search for meanings that may attach with psychic activities of various sorts whereas literary criticism does not always look for meanings. It is sometimes testified by responsible poets and critics that literary works of great merit need not always mean: *A poem,* says Archibald MacLeish, "should not mean/But be" (cited in Wimsatt & Brooks 1964: 249). Perhaps it is valid to say that best poetry is half understood. And it is here that the open-endedness of Jung's thinking is most evident. He wonders if art really *means* anything at all: "perhaps art has no *meaning,* at least, not as we understand meaning. Perhaps it is like nature, which simply *is* and means nothing beyond that .... Art, it has been said, is beauty, and "a thing of beauty is a joy forever". It needs no meaning, for "meaning has nothing to do with art" (1966: 77). Having quoted Oscar Wilde's mischievous dictum that a work of art is something entirely *useless,* Jung seems to point out in his remarkable essay on *Ulysses* that the best use of art arises from its apparent *uselessness* (cf p 113). In his letter to James Joyce (in 1934) Jung writes: "I shall probably never be quite sure whether I did enjoy it (*Ulysses*), because it meant too much grinding of nerves and of grey matter. I don't know whether you will enjoy what I have written about *Ulysses* because I couldn't help telling the world how much I was bored, how I grumbled, how I cursed and how I admired" (*ibid,* p 134). In response to his letter Joyce inscribed the following remarks on the fly-leaf of Jung's copy of *Ulysses*: "To Dr C G Jung with grateful appreciation of his aid and counsel. James Joyce X-mas 1934. Zurich" (*ibid,* p 134).

**Art and Private Life**

Jung's emphatic denial of there being any logical link between the work of art and the private life of the artist stands in direct opposition to the central tenet of Freudian poetics. There is, Jung contends, no justification for judging a work of art by personal criteria because it is something "suprapersonal". Indeed, the special significance of a work of art lies in the fact that it has "escaped from the limitations of the personal and has soared beyond the personal concerns of its creator" (*ibid*, p 71). Jung points out that the essence of a work of art is not to be found in the personal idiosyncracies that creep into it—indeed the more there are of them, the less it is a work of art—but in its rising above the personal and speaking from the mind and heart of the artist to the mind and heart of mankind. Every creative person is a synthesis of contradictions. On the one hand, he is a human being with a personal life, while on the other, he is an impersonal creative process. A great artist is not a person "endowed with free will who seeks his own ends, but one who allows art to realize its purposes through him. As a human being he may have moods and a will and personal aim, but as an artist he is "man" in a higher sense, he is "collective man", "a vehicle and moulder of the unconscious psychic life of mankind" (*ibid*, p 101). We cannot draw reliable inferences about the work of art from the life of the artist or about the life of the artist from the work of art because the two are not usually connected. The personal approach cannot be helpful for the analysis of poetry because the emotion of art, on Eliot's testimony, is impersonal. The poet cannot reach this impersonality without surrendering himself wholly to the work to be done (cf Eliot 1972). Eliot, like Jung, maintains that during the process of creation the artist is called upon to give himself completely to the creative process: "The progress of an artist is a continual self-sacrifice, a continual extinction of personality" (*ibid*). The creative process may partly or exclusively operate upon the experience of the man himself, but "the more perfect the artist, the more completely separate in him will be the man who suffers and the mind which creates" (*ibid*). The creative process, Jung argues, is "a thing and not a personality: hence it cannot be judged by personal criteria" (1966: 71).

**Role of the Psychologist**

If we were to ask what specific contributions the psychologist as psychologist could make to the study of literature, Jung would make two modest claims. First he would say that the psychologist can certainly tell us a good deal about the nature of the creative process and about the relation of the creative writer to the creative process. The psychologist as psychologist, Jung clarifies, cannot tell us anything about the relative artistic value of a work of art, —although we can definitely benefit from the psychologist's knowledge about man's creative processes or forms of symbolization, myths, and the great immemorial symbols—the primordial images or the archetypes in which men in general and artists in particular tend to express themselves (cf Jung 1966, pp 65-66 & Wimsatt & Brooks 1964: 719-20).

Jung's second claim relates to his historic distinction between what he calls "the two modes of artistic creation": the *Psychological* and the *Visionary*. The psychological mode works with materials drawn from the artist's conscious experience and intention. The artist wants to fulfil his aim. He selects his material from crucial experiences, powerful emotions and extraordinary situations and transmutes them into an artistic whole which we all like and enjoy. There is, in most of such works, a visible correlation of the artist to his work. In all such works the artist is so clearly identifiable that "his intentions and his faculties are indistinguishable from the act of creation itself" (Jung 1966: 72). Such works constitute the vast majority of artistic compositions. Since no obscurity surrounds them, for they fully explain themselves in their own terms, there is "no work left for the psychologist to do"(*ibid*, p 89).

In dealing with psychological works of art, Jung assures us, we need never ask ourselves what the material consists of or what it means because there is nothing vague or obscure about them (p 91). But as soon as we encounter visionary works, questions like these burst on our face because we do not know where we stand. We are "astonished, confused, bewildered, put on our guard or even repelled; we demand commentaries and explanations. We are reminded of nothing in everyday life, but rather of dreams, night-time fears, and the dark, uncanny recesses of the human mind" (p 91). In the domain of the visionary mode of creation the artist is no longer free, his sense of freedom turns out to be an illusion: "he fancies he is swimming, but in reality an unseen current sweeps him along" (p 74). The biographies of great artists, Jung points out, make it abundantly clear that the creative urge is so imperious that "it battens on their humanity and yokes everything to the service of the work, even at the cost of health and ordinary human happiness. The unborn work in the psyche of the artist is a force of nature that achieves its end either with tyrannical might or with the subtle cunning of nature herself, quite regardless of the personal fate of the man who is its vehicle. The creative urge lives and grows in him like a tree in the earth from which it draws its nourishment. We would do well, therefore, to think of the creative process as a living thing implanted in the psyche. In the language of analytical psychology this living thing is an *autonomous complex*" (p 75) The author of the visionary work is called upon to surrender his individual identity completely to the work in hand because at such moments he becomes, willy-nilly, one with humanity. "Whoever speaks", writes Jung, "in primordial images speaks with a thousand voices; he enthrals and overpowers, while at the same time he lifts the idea he is seeking to express out of the occasional and the transitory into the realm of the ever-enduring. He transmutes our personal destiny into the destiny of mankind, and evokes in us all those beneficent forces that ever and anon have enabled humanity to find a refuge from every peril and to outlive the longest night" (p 82). As far as the visionary mode is concerned, neither the critic nor the psychologist can hope to find any link between the private life of the artist and the content of his work. He cannot even trust the author himself if he tells us that there is because what he may say about such link is often far from being the best word on the subject. Jung goes to the extent of saying: "It seems as if we have to defend the seriousness of the visionary experience against the personal resistance of the poet himself" (p 94).

**Jung: A Remarkable Personality**

Perhaps no great thinker of our century has been held in more varied esteem than Jung. Critical opinions about him have been fluctuating from unqualified glorification to systematic hostility. Unsympathetic critics generally treat the concept of the Collective Unconscious as a "sentimental derivative of ancestor worship" (Glover in Woodworth 1965: 312), "a welcome escape from the rigors of science" (Chafe 1974), "a mish-mash of Oriental philosophy with a bowdlerised psychology" (Glover in Dry 1961: X) and "so mysterious as to be almost undiscussable" (Peters *ibid*, p XI). Enthusiastic supporters, on the other hand, eulogize Jung's contribution to psychology as revolutionary. Baynes, for instance, describes the later ideas of Jung as psychological explosives which can affect human life "as profoundly as the release of the atomic energy" (quoted in Dry 1961: IX). Neumann believes Jung's work to be the "grandest attempt yet made to construct *a theory of the Psyche*" while Priestley thinks that Jung is not only "one of the great original thinkers of our time but also one of its few liberators" (*ibid*, pp IX-X).

In between these extreme views lies a point of view which tries to be as objective and moderate as possible but even this point of view varies from an attitude of indifference to a feeling of bewilderment. Most people who have attempted a critical assessment of Jung's writings have come to the conclusion that "he contradicts himself, uses words in differing senses and often makes use of `blanket' concepts which include so much under a single heading that they actually explain less than at first appears" (Storr 1973: 79). One can easily point out terminological inaccuracies in Jung's writings. A ready example is his opposition between the *Psychological* and the *Visionary* modes of artistic creation. This opposition could have been better described by some such contrast as literalistic vs apocalyptic, commonplace vs sublime, pedestrian vs visionary, individualistic vs cosmic or personalistic vs universalistic. Jung himself seems to have been aware of such difficulties. As he says: "nobody reads my books ... I have such a hell of a trouble to make people to see what I mean" (*ibid*, 106). However, credit must be given to Jung for having made available a new perspective of thinking for students of literary criticism. It is very likely that some of his concepts and ideas are non-scientific but it is undeniable that he has something remarkable to say about the structure of artistic experiences. A major argument in favour of the Collective Unconscious could be, as a distinguished psychologist claimed more than half century ago, that "there are easily recognizable resemblances among the primitive legends of peoples widely separated throughout the world, even though there have been no known means of inter-communication" (Woodworth 1965: 312).

# Works Cited


Abrams, M H (1971), *The Mirror and the Lamp: Romantic Theory and the Critical Tradition*, Oxford, Oxford University Press, First Published in 1953.

——— (1978), *A Glossary of Literary Terms*, Delhi, The Macmillan Company of India.

Ahmad, K, *Psychoanalysis and Literary Criticism*, Patna: Shri Ajanta Press.

Anandavardhana, (1982), *Dhvanyaloka*, ed K Krishnamoorthy, Delhi, Motilal Banarsidass.

Aristotle, (1946), *The Works of Aristotle*, Vol IX, *Ethica Nicomachea*, ed W D Ross, Oxford, At the Clarendon Press.

———, *The Works of Aristotle*, Vol XI, (*De Rhetorica, De Poetica*), ed W D Ross, Oxford, At the Clarendon Press.

———, *The Politics of Aristotle*, ed Earnest Barker, Oxford, Oxford University Press.

——— (1968), *Aristotle's Poetics*, ed by Leon Golden and Commentary by O B Hardison Jr, Englewood Cliffs & New Jersey, Prentice Hall.

Arnold, Matthew (1960), *Culture and Anarchy*, ed J Dover Wilson Cambridge, Cambridge University Press, Originally Published in 1869.

Asimov, Isaac (1975), *Asimov's Guide to Science*, Vol 2, *The Biological Sciences*, Harmondsworth, Penguin Books.

Auden, W H (1973), 'In Memory of Sigmund Freud' in *Freud*, ed Frank Cioffi, pp 57-60.

Bhamah, (1970), *Kavyalankar*, ed P V N Shastri,Delhi, Motilal Banarsidass.

Bharatamuni, (1972, 1978, 1983), *Natyashastra*, ed B L S Shastri, Vols I-III, Varanasi, Chawkhambha Sanskrit Sansthan.

Blum, G S (1969), *Psychodynamics: The Science of Unconscious Mental Processes*, New Delhi, Prentice-Hall of India.

Bodkin, Maud (1963), *Archetypal Patterns in Poetry*, London, Oxford University Press, First Published in 1934.

Brander, L (1963), ed *Window on the World*, Madras, Oxford University Press.

Bridges, Robert (1933), 'Poetic Diction' in *English Critical Essays*, First series, ed P M Jones, pp 1-10, London, Oxford University Press, First Published in *The Forum*, May 1923.

Brown, J A C (1961), *Freud and the Post-Freudians*, Harmondsworth, Penguin Books.

Bruner, J S (1973), 'Freud and the Image of man' in *Freud*, ed Frank Cioffi, pp 138-45.

Burke, Kenneth (1973), *The Philosophy of Literary Form*, London, University of California Press, First published in 1941 by Lousiana University Press.

Bywater, Ingram (1946), trans *De Poetica* in *The Works of Aristotle*, ed W D Ross, Vol XI, London, At the Clarendon Press.

__________, 'Catharsis' in *Encyclopaedia Britanica*, Micropaedia, Vol 2, p 639.

Chase, Richard (1974), 'Notes on the Study of Myth' in *Twentieth-Century Criticism*, ed W J Handy and M Westbrook, New Delhi, Light & Life Publishers.

Chatterjee, S and Datta, D (1960), *An Introduction to Indian Philosophy*, Calcutta, University of Calcutta, First published in 1939.

Chatterji, S K (1978), *Select Writings*, New Delhi : Vikas Publishing House, Vol I.

Christophersen, Paul (1973), *Second Language Learning*, Harmondsworth, Penguin Books.

Cioffi, Frank (1973), ed *Freud*, London, Macmillan.

————, 'Introduction' to *Freud*, ed Frank Cioffi, pp 1-24.

Conversi, L W (1980), 'Tragedy' in *Encyclopaedia Britannica*, Macro, Vol 18, pp 580-92.

Daiches, David (1956), *Critical Approaches to Literature*, New Delhi, Orient Longman.

Dalal, Minakshi (1973), *Conflict in Sanskrit Drama*, Bombay, Somaiya Publications.

Dandin (1973), *Kavyadarsha*, ed D K Gupta, Delhi, Meharchand Lakshmandas.

Das, Bhagwan (1949), *Ancient Psychosynthesis Versus Modern Psycho-Analysis*, Madras, The Theosophical Publishing House.

Dasgupta, S N (1970), 'The Theory of Rasa' *An Introduction to Indian Poetics*, ed V Raghavan and Nagendra, Bombay, Macmillan & Co, pp 36-41.

Davies, J T (1965), *The Scientific Method*, London, Academic Press.

De, S K (1959), *Some Problems of Sanskrit Poetics*, Calcutta, Firma K L M.

Dorius, R J (1965), 'Tragedy' in *Princeton Encyclopedia of Poetry and Poetics*, Princeton, The University Press, pp 860-64.

Dorsh, T S (1965), ed *Classical Literary Criticism*, Harmondsworth, Penguin Books.

Dry, A M (1961), *The Psychology of Jung*, London, Metheun & Co Ltd.

Dryden, John (1976), *Absalom and Achitophel*, ed James and Helen Kinsley, Delhi, Oxford University Press.

Duke, M H (1972), *Sigmund Freud*, London, Lutterworth Press.

Eliot, T S (1953), *Selected Prose*, Harmondsworth, Penguin Press.

———— (1958), *Little Gidding* in *The Faber Book of English*

*Verse*, London, Faber and Faber, pp 436-43.

Eliot, T S (1972), 'Tradition and Individual Talent' in *20th Century Literary Criticism*, ed David Lodge, pp 71-77, London, Longman, The essay was first published in 1919.

__________, 'Decorum' (1980), in *Encyclopaedia Britannica*, Micropaedia, Vol III, p 428.

Evans, R I (1964), *Conversations with Jung*, New York, London, Van Nostrand, Reinhold Company.

Fraiberg, Louis (1974), *Psychoanalysis and American Literary Criticism*, New York, Octagon Books, First Published in 1960.

Fries, C C (1945), *Teaching and Learning English as a Foreign Language*, Ann Arbor, University of Michigan Press.

Freud, S (1938), *Basic Writings of Sigmund Freud*, Trans A A Brill, New York, The Modern Library.

__________ (1963), 'Civilization and Its Discontent' in *Window on the World*, ed L Brander, pp 29-40, The essay was first published in 1930 as part of Freud's book of the same name.

__________ (1964), *New Introductory Lectures on Psychoanalysis*, New York, Norton.

__________ (1972), 'Creative Writers and Day-Dreaming' in *20th Century Literary Criticism*, ed David Lodge, pp 36-42, The essay was first published in 1908.

__________ (1976), *Jokes and Their Relation to the Unconscious*, ed Angela Richards, Harmondsworth, Penguin Books, First published in 1905 under the title *Wit and Its Relation to the Unconscious*.

Fromm, Eric (1970), *The Crisis of Psychoanalysis*, Harmondsworth, Penguin Books.

Gilbert, A H (1970), 'Decorum' in *Dictionary of World Literary Terms*, ed J T Shipley, London, George Allen & Unwin, pp 76-77.

Gnoli, R (1970), 'The Aesthetic Experience According to Abhinavagupta' in *An Introduction to Indian Poetics*, ed Raghavan & Nagendra, pp 75-81.

Golden, Leon & Hardison Jr, O B (1968), eds *Aristotle's Poetics*, Englewood Cliffs & New Jersey, Prentice Hall.

Greer, Germaine (1973), *The Female Eunuch*, New York, Bantam Books.

Grun, Barnard (1975), *The Time Tables of History*, London, Thames and Hudson.

Guerin, W L *et al* (1979), eds *A Handbook of Critical Approaches to Literature*, New York, London, Harper & Row.

Hadas, M (1951), *The Basic Works of Cicero*, New York, The Modern Library, 'Introduction', pp IX-XXI.

Hall, Vernon (1963), *A Short History of Literary Criticism*, London, The Merlin Press.

Handy, W J and Westbrook, M (1974), eds *Twentieth-Century Criticism*, New Delhi, Light & Life Publishers.

Hardison Jr, O B (1968), Commentary on *Aristotle's Poetics*, ed Leon Golden.

Herrick, M T (1965), 'Decorum' in *Princeton Encyclopedia of Poetry and Poetics*, ed Alex Preminger, pp 187-88.

Horace (1936), *The Complete Works*, ed C J Kramaer, New York, The Modern Library.

Hospers, J (1980), 'Philosophy of Art' in *Encyclopaedia Britannica*, Macropaedia, Vol 2, pp 40-56.

Iyengar, K R S (1973), *Indian Writing in English*, Bombay, Asia Publishing House, First published in 1962.

Jastrow, J (1949), *Freud : His Dream and Sex Theories*, Allahabad, Central Book Depot.

Jones, Ernest (1964), *The Life and Work of Sigmund Freud*, eds L Trilling and S Marcus, Harmondsworth, Penguin Books, Originally Published in 3 Vols by Hogarth Press in 1953-57 under the title: *Sigmund Freud : Life and Works*.

———— (1974), 'Hamlet: The Psychoanalytical Solution' in *Twentieth-Century Criticism*, eds Handy & Westbrook, pp 484-99.

Jung, C G (1963), 'The Spiritual Problem of Modern Man' in

*Window on the World*, ed L Brander, pp 42-68.

Jung, C G (1966), *The Collected Works*, Vol 15, Trans R F C Hull London & Henley, Routledge & Kegan Paul.

———— (1967), *Memories, Dreams, Reflections*, Trans R & C Winston, London & Glasgow, Collins.

———— (1972), 'Psychology and Literature' in *20th Century Literary Criticism*, ed David Lodge, pp 175-88.

———— (1973), 'Sigmund Freud in Historical Perspective' in *Freud*, ed Frank Cioffi, pp 49-56.

———— (1974), 'Archetypes of the Collective Unconsciousness' in *Twentieth-Century Criticism*, ed Handy & Westbrook, pp 205-32. The essay was originally published in Vol 9 of *The Collected Works*, in 1959.

Kane, P V (1971), *History of Sanskrit Poetics*, Delhi, Motilal Banarsidass.

Keith, A B (1924), *The Sanskrit Drama*, London, Oxford University Press.

Kshemendra, (1982), *Auchityavicharcharcha*, ed R S Tripathi, Varanasi, Krishnadas Sanskrit Academy.

Kuhn, Thomas (1970), *The Structure of Scientific Revolutions*, Chicago, The University of Chicago Press, First Published in 1963.

Kuntaka, (1977), *Vakroktijivita*, ed K Krishnamoorthy Dharwar, Karnataka University.

LaDriere, J C (1970), 'Fitness' and 'Decorum' in *Dictionary of World Literary Terms*, ed J T Shipley, pp 121-22, 127-31, London, George Allen & Unwin.

Lodge, David (1972), ed *20th Century Literary Criticism*, London, Longman, 'Editorial Note on Jung', p 174.

Macalpine, Ida (1973), 'Tribute to Freud' in *Freud*, ed Frank Cioffi, pp 124-37.

Magee, Bryan (1973), *Popper*, London, Fontana/Collins, Modern Masters.

Mann, Thomas (1973), 'Freud and the Future' in *Freud*, ed

Frank Cioffi, pp 57-75.

McGlashan, A M & Reeve, C G (1970), *Freud*, London, Rupert Hart-Davis Educational Publishers.

Mckeon, R (1957), 'Literary Criticism and the Concept of Imitation in Antiquity' in *Critics and Criticism*, ed R S Crane, Chicago & London, The University of Chicago Press, Abridged edition, pp 117-45.

Milton, John (1954), *The Reason of Church Government*, ed C A Patrides in *John Milton: Selected Prose*, Harmondsworth, Penguin Books.

———— (1957), *Complete Poems and Major Prose*, ed M Y Hughes, Delhi, The Bobbs-Merrill Educational Publishing Company.

———— (1960), *Samson Agonistes*, ed M D Davis, London, Macmillan.

Morrison, Claudia (1968), *Freud and the Critic*, Chapel Hill, The University of North Carolina Press.

Mukherji, R (1966), *Literary Criticism in Ancient India*, Calcutta, Sanskrit Pustak Bhandar.

Muller, F Max (1964), *The Sacred Books of the East*, Vol XXV, *The Laws of Manu*, Delhi, Motilal Banarsidass, First Published in 1886.

Nagendra (1970), 'The Nature of Aesthetic Experience' in *An Introduction to Indian Poetics*, ed Raghavan and Nagendra, pp 117-27.

Palmer, O J (1973), 'Decorum' in *A Dictionary of Modern Critical Terms*, ed Roger Fowler, London, Routledge & Kegan Paul, p 48.

Pepper, S C (1980), 'Aesthetics' in *Encyclopaedia Britannica*, Macro, Vol 1, pp 149-62.

Plato, (1961), *The Collected Works of Plato*, eds E Hamilton & H Cairns, Princeton, The University of Princeton Press.

Pollard, Arthur (1970), *Satire*, London, Metheun, The Critical Idiom Series.

Raghavan, V (1965), 'Indian Poetics' in *Princeton Encyclopedia of Poetry and Poetics*, pp 383-84.

——— (1970), 'Auchitya in Sanskrit Poetics' in *An Introduction to Indian Poetics*, eds V Raghavan and Nagendra, pp 102-16, Madras, Macmillan Company.

Rahula, Walpole (1980), 'Buddha' in *Encyclopaedia Britannica*, Macro, Vol 3, pp 369-74.

Rangacharya, Adya (1966), *Introduction to Bharata's Natyashastra*, Bombay, Popular Prakashan.

Read, Herbert (1974), 'Psychoanalysis and Criticism' in *Twentieth-Century Criticism*, eds Handy and Westbrook, pp 419-29.

Richards, Angela (1976), 'Editorial Note' on Freud's *Jokes and Their Relation to the Unconscious*, pp 11-24.

Richards, I A (1960), *Principles of Literary Criticism*, London, Routledge & Kegan Paul, First Published in 1924.

——— (1965), *The Philosophy of Rhetoric*, New York, Oxford University Press, First Published in 1936.

——— (1966), 'Introduction' to *Plato's Republic*, ed I A Richards, Cambridge, The University Press, pp 1-13.

Riesman, David (1973), 'The Themes of Work and Play in the Structure of Freud's Thought' in *Sigmund Freud*, ed Paul Roazen, pp 118-41.

Riviere, Jacques (1973), 'The Three Main Theses of Psychoanalysis' in *Freud*, ed Frank Cioffi, pp 25-41.

Roazen, Paul (1973), 'Introduction' to *Sigmund Freud*, ed Paul Roazen, pp 1-29, Englewood Cliffs, New Jersey, Prentice Hall.

Robert, M (1966), *The Psychoanalytic Revolution*, London, George Allen & Unwin.

Robins, R H (1967), *A Short History of Linguistics*, London, Harlow, Longmans, Green & Co.

Rogerson, B (1965), 'Types of Criticism' in *Princeton Encyclopedia of Poetry and Poetics*, pp 163-74.

Rudd, Niall (1973), ed *Horace : Satires and Epistles*, Harmondsworth, Penguin Books, 'Introduction', pp 9-35.

Rudrata (1966), *Kavyalankar*, ed R Shukla Varanasi, The Chawkhambha Sanskrit Series.

Sankaran, A (1973), *Some Aspects of Literary Criticism in Sanskrit*, New Delhi, Oriental Books, First Published in 1926.

Santayana, George (1973), 'A Long Way Round to Nirvana' in *Freud*, ed Frank Cioffi, pp 42-48.

Schorer, Mark (1972), 'Technique as Discovery' *20th Century Literary Criticism*, ed David Lodge, The essay was first published in 1948.

Shakespeare, William (1971), *A Midsummer Night's Dream*, ed M Doran, Harmondsworth, Penguin Books.

Sharma, R P (1979), *I A Richards' Theory of Language*, New Delhi, S Chand and Company.

Shastri, S Kuppuswami (1970), 'The High-Ways of Literary Criticism in Sanskrit' in *An Introduction to Indian Poetics*, ed Raghavan and Nagendra, pp 20-35.

Shastri, B L S (1972), ed *Natyashastra*, Vol 1, 1978, Vols 2-3, 1983, Varanasi, Chawkhambha Sanskrit Series.

Shaw, G B (1946), *Man and Superman*, Harmondsworth, Penguin Books, first Published in 1903.

Shreemali, N D (1948), *Ank Jyotish*, Delhi, Anand Paperbacks.

Sidney, Philip (1975), *An Apology for Poetry*, ed V Chatterjee, Calcutta, Orient Longman.

Shipley, J T (1970), ed *Dictionary of World Literary Terms*, London, George Allen & Unwin.

Storr, A (1973), *Jung*, London, Fontana/Collins, Modern Masters.

————, *The Bhagavadgita*, trans & ed S Radhakrishnan (1971), Bombay, Blackie and Son (India) Ltd.

————, *The Holy Bible*, King James Version.

————, *The Manusmriti*, Trans & Commentary by Narayan Ram, 1946, Bombay, Satyabhamabai Pandurang.

Storr, A, *The McGraw Hill Encyclopaedia of World Biography*, (1973), London, New York, McGraw Hill Book Co.

Trilling, L (1964), 'Introduction' to *The Life and Work of Sigmund Freud*, by Ernest Jones, pp 11-24.

——— (1970), *The Liberal Imagination*, Harmondsworth, Penguin Books, first published in 1940.

——— (1980), *The Opposing Self*, London, Oxford University Press, first published in 1955.

Vaman (1971), *Kavyalankarsutra*, ed B Jha Varanasi, Chawkhambha Sanskrit Series.

Vivekananda, Swami (1964), *Jnanayoga*, Calcutta, Advaita Ashram.

——— (1968), *Complete Works*, Vol 6, Calcutta, Advaita Ashram.

Waith, E M (1972), 'Dryden and the Tradition of Serious Drama' in *John Dryden*, ed Earl Miner, London, G Bells & Sons, pp 58-89.

Warner, Alan (1962), *A Short Guide to English Style*, London, ELBS.

Wellek, R and Warren, A (1956), *Theory of Literature*, Harmondsworth, Penguin Books, First Published in 1949.

Wheelwright, Philip (1965), 'Catharsis' in *Princeton Encyclopedia of Poetry and Poetics*, pp 106-8.

Wilkinson, L P (1968), *Horace and His Lyric Poetry*, Cambridge, Cambridge University Press.

Wimsatt Jr, W K and Brooks, C (1964), *Literary Criticism: A Short History*, New Delhi, Oxford & I B H Publishing Co., First Published in 1957.

Wittgenstein, L (1973), 'Conversations on Freud' in *Freud*, ed Frank Cioffi, pp 76-86.

Woodworth, R S (1965), *Contemporary Schools of Psychology*, London, Metheun & Co Ltd, first published in 1931.

Wollheim, Richard (1971), *Freud*, Glasgow, Fontana, Modern Masters.

# Index